BRUCE NORRIS

Bruce Norris is the author of *Clybourne Park*, which premiered in 2010 at Playwrights Horizons (New York) and received the Pulitzer Prize for Drama, as well as the Olivier, Evening Standard, and Tony Awards. In 2017 he adapted Brecht's *Arturo Ui* for the Donmar Warehouse, and in 2018 *The Low Road* (which opened at the Royal Court Theatre in 2013) was seen at the Public Theatre, New York. Other plays include *The Qualms*, *Domesticated*, *A Parallelogram*, *The Unmentionables*, *The Pain and the Itch*, and *Purple Heart,* many of which premiered at Steppenwolf Theatre, Chicago, where he is an ensemble member. He lives in New York.

D1214910

Bruce Norris

DOWNSTATE

NICK HERN BOOKS

London

www.nickhernbooks.co.uk

A Nick Hern Book

Downstate first published in Great Britain in 2019 as a paperback original by Nick Hern Books Limited, The Glasshouse, 49a Goldhawk Road, London W12 8QP

Downstate copyright © 2019 Bruce Norris

Bruce Norris has asserted his right to be identified as the author of this work

Front cover: Image by Michael Cranston

Designed and typeset by Nick Hern Books, London
Printed in Great Britain by Mimeo Ltd, Huntingdon, Cambridgeshire PE29 6XX

A CIP catalogue record for this book is available from the British Library

ISBN 978 1 84842 819 5

Woodland
CARBON
www.woodlandcarbon.co.uk
NICK HERN BOOKS
Printed on Carbon Captured paper

Downstate was co-commissioned and its world premiere was presented by Steppenwolf Theatre Company, Chicago (Anna Shapiro, Artistic Director; David Schmitz, Executive Director) and the National Theatre, London (Rufus Norris, Artistic Director; Lisa Burger, Executive Director).

Downstate premiered on 30 September 2018, at Steppenwolf's Upstairs Theatre, Chicago, and opened on 20 March 2019 in the Dorfman auditorium of the National Theatre, London. The cast, in alphabetical order, was as follows:

COPS (Chicago)	Elyakeem Avraham
	Maura Kidwell
	Nate Whelden
GIO	Glenn Davis
COPS (London)	Mark Extance
	Brinsley Terence
	Shelley Williams
DEE	K. Todd Freeman
FRED	Francis Guinan
ANDY	Tim Hopper
IVY	Cecilia Noble
FELIX	Eddie Torres
EFFIE	Aimee Lou Wood
EM	Matilda Ziegler

Director	Pam MacKinnon
Set Designer	Todd Rosenthal
Costume Designer	Clint Ramos
Lighting Designer	Adam Silverman
Sound Designer	Carolyn Downing
Vocal Coach	Gigi Buffington
Staff Director	Eva Sampson
Stage Manager (*Chicago*)	Laura Glenn
Assistant Stage Manager (*Chicago*)	Christine D. Freeburg
Stage Manager (*London*)	Alison Rankin
Deputy Stage Manager (*London*)	Fiona Bardsley
Assistant Stage Manager (*London*)	Abigail Thornton

For Martha Lavey

Characters

ANDY, *late thirties–forties, white, professional*
EM, *late thirties–forties, same as Andy*
FRED, *seventies, white, glasses, motorized wheelchair,*
    childlike, not unlike Fred Rogers
DEE, *pushing sixty, black, thin, languid*
GIO, *thirties, black, muscular, clean-cut, ambitious, voluble*
FELIX, *forties, Latino, heavyset, solitary, silent*
IVY, *forties–fifties, black or Latina, Probation officer –*
    overworked, weary
EFFIE, *late teens – early twenties. Any ethnicity. Hyperactive.*
    Too much eye make-up
COPS (*non-speaking*), *two male, one female, to be played by*
    understudies

Setting

A group home for sex offenders, downstate Illinois: a single-story house, built in the 1950s or '60s, now deteriorated. Superficial attempts have been made to make the place livable but they fail to relieve the general dreariness of the place. Ugly contemporary sofa, small flat-screen TV, second-hand dining table and chairs, window-unit AC. One broken window, repaired with duct tape and cardboard. In one corner, a weight-training bench with barbells. In another, an electric keyboard. An aluminium baseball bat leans next to the front door. Kitchen partially visible through a doorway. A hall leads to a bathroom and bedrooms. To the rear of the main room, an accordion door has been added to create a fourth bedroom from an alcove. When the door opens we can see into Felix's cramped room: single bed, crucifix upon the wall, personal items, mini-fridge, etc.

No music should be used in the play except as indicated.

The time is the present.

This text went to press before the end of rehearsals and so may differ slightly from the play as performed.

ACT ONE

June. Saturday morning. Warm outside. Windows closed, shades drawn. A window unit hums feebly.

ANDY and EM together on sofa, opposite FRED in his wheelchair. ANDY stares at some printed pages in his lap. EM looks at him expectantly. Long pause. She places a hand on his knee.

[handwritten margin note: lack of power @ present]

EM. Ready?

ANDY nods, clears his throat.

ANDY. For a number of years –

[handwritten margin note: What role is em playing? advocate?]

EM. Take your time.

ANDY (*calm, measured*). For a number of years I told myself my life was good. And to the casual observer, this would appear to be true: I have a loving partner, I have a family, I have a home. And as long as I *told* myself this story, I believed it, too: Life was good and the past was the past and had no power over me in the present. (*Beat.*) But after my child was b–

His voice catches. EM touches him.

(*Very quietly.*) Sorry.

EM (*whisper*). You're okay.

ANDY (*whisper*). I'm fine.

EM (*whisper*). Proud of you.

Another deep breath. He resumes.

ANDY. But after my child was born I started having panic attacks. And at first I didn't want to make the association. I kept telling myself that fear and anxiety were *normal* responses to parenthood, what *any* adult would naturally feel when faced with the responsibility of caring for an innocent life. But then I started to notice that other parents were *not* anxious, on the contrary, they seemed happy and fulfilled. And it was only then I began to accept that we can never truly escape the past, and that evil exists in the world, and for me, at this moment, one part of that acceptance, is to look you in the eye today, and tell you to your face that you are a fundamentally evil person.

EM *nods, gravely.*

FRED (*gently*). Are you sure you don't want some coffee?

EM. He's not finished.

FRED. Sorry.

EM. Let's let him finish.

FRED. Okay.

ANDY *takes a breath, continues reading.*

ANDY. I used to fantasize about how I would kill you.

FRED. Okay.

ANDY (*calmly*). I would park outside your apartment and wait until you pulled in the driveway. And I would bring along my mother's .38, the one she kept in her bedside table, and when you stepped out of your car I would hold it against your head and duct tape your mouth so I wouldn't have to listen to any of your toxic bullshit –

FRED. Sure.

ANDY. – and I'd drive you to the edge of the forest preserve, and you'd kneel down in the dirt –

EM*'s cell begins to ring. She glances at the screen.*

– and I'd rip the tape off your mouth and jam the barrel of the gun down your throat, so that you – so that you might – (*Noticing phone, to* EM.) you wanna – ?

EM answers her phone.

EM (*sotto*). What's up?

ANDY and FRED stare at the floor.

Okay, but what did we say about the whiny voice? Yes, much better. Thank you. (*Beat.*) I don't know. Maybe forty-five minutes?

ANDY gestures apologetically to FRED.

Well, where's the charger? Did you look in the zippy bag? Okay, then have Maria take you to the front desk maybe they have a charger.

ANDY. There's games on the TV.

EM. Daddy says they have games on the TV.

ANDY. *Smash Brothers*.

EM. Daddy says they have *Smash Brothers*.

A bedroom door opens in the hall. GIO briefly appears in sweatpants and a tank top. He inconspicuously enters the bathroom, closing the door behind him. ANDY notices.

Yeah ask Maria to set you up with *Smash Brothers* and by the time you're finished we'll be back. Tell her charge it to the room.

ANDY (*to* FRED). Sorry.

FRED. No no.

ANDY. Taking him to the water park.

FRED. That sounds like fun.

EM (*on phone*). Well, what did I just say? Soon as we get back to the hotel, okay? Okay. (*She hangs up. To* ANDY.) Sorry.

ANDY looks for his place in the letter.

ANDY (*to* FRED). Um. I don't remember what I –

FRED. The gun in my –

ANDY. – Right. Right.

> ANDY *finds where he left off, clears throat.*

> (*Reading.*) ...and I'd jam the – it's a *fantasy*, you know –

FRED. I know that.

ANDY. – it's a way of communicating some sense of of of the –

EM (*overlapping*). You don't have to explain.

ANDY (*continuous*). – emotional cost of what – I'm not.

EM. Or justify.

ANDY. – I didn't – it's just – (*To* FRED.) sometimes it's difficult for me to be um, you know, totally direct so this is a way of –

EM (*overlapping*). But why are you backpedalling?

ANDY (*continuous*). – unambiguously – (*To* EM.) I'm *not*.

EM. This is what you *feel*, and you have *ownership* of those feelings –

ANDY. I know that.

EM. – whether it makes him uncomfortable or not. (*To* FRED.) Right?

FRED. That's right.

EM. And if it does? So be it.

ANDY. I agree.

EM. So let's do what we're here to do, okay?

ANDY. Right. Okay.

> ANDY *scans the page.*

> Um. So I'm gonna skip ahead to –

FRED. Okay.

ANDY (*to himself, finding his place*)....um, the guilt and the shame you forced me to live with... (*Aloud.*) by exploiting my trust. By enlisting my sympathy. But you will never be deserving of sympathy –

The front door opens. DEE enters from outside: sunglasses, flip-flops. He wheels a creaky metal shopping cart filled with groceries through the room en route to the kitchen. Once he is gone, ANDY continues.

(*Reading.*) – you will never be deserving of sympathy, or forgiveness. That is not something I can –

DEE now crosses from the kitchen to the bathroom, finds it locked, knocks lightly. No answer. He waits by the door. ANDY hesitates again.

EM (*prompting* ANDY)....not something you can – ?

ANDY (*reading*). That is not something I can give you. But I must remember to forgive *myself*, and remember that I was only a child, and to treat myself with the same respect and loving kindness that any child deserves.

In the hallway, DEE knocks again at the closed bathroom door.

GIO. I'll be out when I'm out.

DEE folds his arms, waits. Brief pause.

FRED (*to* ANDY). So is that it? Is there any more, or – ?

ANDY. That's – No. I mean – Yeah. That's it. That's all.

Silence. EM rubs ANDY's back, comforting.

FRED. Well gosh, you know... it just makes me so sad to –

EM. Sorry.

FRED. Whoops.

EM. I have a letter.

FRED. Okay.

ANDY. She has one too.

FRED. Okay.

EM *unfolds a letter from her pocket, reads.*

EM. I. Am a mother. And a wife. And a daughter and a granddaughter and a sister and a niece. But first and foremost I am a mother. And however strong the love I feel for my husband, that love will always be secondary to that which I feel for my child.

ANDY (*nodding*). As it should.

EM. And if they were trapped in a burning building, and I had only strength to rescue one of them, there is no question which one that would be.

ANDY (*nodding vigorously*). Right. Right.

EM. But how can I ever explain to my child why Daddy is sometimes sad? Why he'd rather sit alone in the dark instead of using the PlayStation? Children need answers. And they need to know that some monsters are real.

Bathroom door opens. GIO *exits as* DEE *quickly enters.* GIO *crosses into the kitchen, with a glance toward the others.* EM *folds her letter.*

And? On a personal note? For me? Having to sit here today? Because I understand that – for Andy – this is an opportunity for a kind of reckoning, and I know we're living through an amazing historical moment, so I want to be supportive, but if I'm being totally honest? Having to sit here with a person who devastated the life of someone I love? Frankly? Makes me want to vomit.

FRED (*beat*). Well, I hope that doesn't happen.

The accordion door opens slightly, silently, and FELIX *peeks out.* ANDY *and* EM *turn.*

Are we bothering you, Felix?

FELIX *silently gestures toward the bathroom.*

I think someone's in there right now.

FELIX *nods, closes accordion door again.*

ANDY (*beat*). Didn't realize there was –

FRED. That's just Felix.

> *Toilet flush.* DEE *exits bathroom, heads toward kitchen, with barely a glance to the others.*

ANDY. Lotta people.

FRED. There's four of us.

ANDY. Right.

FRED. Including myself.

ANDY. Right. It's just – Different from what I –

FRED. Pictured?

ANDY. – expected.

FRED. What were you expecting?

ANDY. I dunno. I dunno. Just –

FRED. Something else.

ANDY. – not this.

FRED. They're not listening.

ANDY. I know. I know that. I just –

> *Through the kitchen door, we hear* GIO *and* DEE *bickering, quietly, but still audible.*

GIO (*sotto*). The fuck's this shit?

DEE (*sotto*). Four dollars and seventy-three cents.

GIO (*sotto*). I ain't paying for that.

DEE (*sotto*). Four dollars and seventy –

GIO (*sotto*). They're fuckin' *green*, bruh.

DEE (*sotto*). I can see that.

GIO (*sotto*). How'm I supposed to eat that?

DEE (*sotto*). Four dollars and seventy-three –

[handwritten margin notes: "lives in the group home", "abused", "who now has kid/s + has come to the home to visit I confront fred with his partner em", "audience / judgment"]

GIO (*sotto*). I ain't gonna eat that shit.

FRED (*full volume*). Um? Gio?

> GIO *emerges from the kitchen, all smiles.*

GIO (*glad-handing, to* ANDY *and* EM). So sorry 'bout that. We're being terribly inconsiderate. I do apologize – as well as for the casual state of my attire.   roommate!/
privacy

FRED. If you can give us just a minute –

GIO (*extending hand to* ANDY). Giovanni Joseph.

ANDY. Hi.

GIO (*and to* EM). How ya doin'?

EM. Fine.

GIO. Anything I can do for you folks?

ANDY. No thanks.   EM. Nope. We're good.

GIO. Gotcher selves all situated?

ANDY. We do.

GIO. All squared away?

ANDY. We're fine.

GIO (*re:* ANDY *'s phone*). Ohh look at that. iPhone X.

ANDY. Yeah.

GIO. Latest generation.

ANDY. Yep.

GIO. That's an outstanding choice.

ANDY. Thanks.

GIO. That's a wise investment.

ANDY. Yep.

GIO. I prefer the Samsung Galaxy myself, but that's a solid piece of technology. Anyway, I'll let ya tend to your business.

ANDY. Thanks.

GIO. Sorry to interrupt.

ANDY. It's okay.

GIO. But y'all lemme know if there's anything ya need.

EM. Thank you.

> GIO *turns to exit, passing* DEE, *who holds out a supermarket receipt.* GIO *subtly – and unseen by the others – gives* DEE *the finger as he exits up the hall.* DEE *returns to the kitchen.* ANDY *is clearly frustrated.*

FRED. Anyway –

ANDY (*losing confidence*). Yeah. I dunno. Um. Maybe this is bad –

EM. What are you doing?

ANDY. – timing, or something – I don't know. It's just – it's nothing like what I –

EM. Want to go somewhere else?

ANDY. No.

EM. Let's go somewhere else.

ANDY. *No.* I just – I just – I just –

EM. *What?*

ANDY. – can you *give* me a second?

FRED. Andy? Um, I don't know if this would be helpful, but – is there anything you'd like *me* to say?

ANDY. No. (*Calmly, slowly.*) Nope. Nope.

FRED. You're sure?

ANDY. Yeah. Yep. Yep.

FRED. Okay.

seems like he's listening well

> *Pause, then:*

EM (*beat, to* FRED). Actually –

ANDY. Actually yes.

EM. Actually there is.

FRED. Okay.

EM. Actually – You never actually admitted to what you *did*.

Pause. FRED *thinks, confused.*

FRED. Really?

ANDY. Not everything.

FRED (*stumped*). Huh.

[handwritten: What do dooly + em want/need?
Why does this matter to them?
In what way does it serve repair?]

EM. Not fully, no.

FRED. Gosh.

EM. So Andy and I would like to give you that opportunity.
  Here and now.

  EM *reaches into a bag, pulls out a manila envelope,*
  withdraws a contract.

FRED (*surprised*). Well golly. I sorta *thought* I did –

ANDY (*calmly*). Nope. Nope. Never.

[handwritten: limit of court produced
justice, lawyers, etc.]

FRED (*continuous, overlapping*). – or the lawyers did, at least –

ANDY (*continuous*). Not fully. Not completely.

FRED (*dubious*). Are you *sure*?

ANDY. I remember *very* specifically every detail of everything
  that *happened* and everything you *said*, and everything you
  omitted. Very vividly.

FRED....long time ago.

EM. Well, not for us.

[handwritten: burdens of
being victim vs.
perpetrator]

FRED. Okay.

EM. We live with the repercussions every single day.

FRED. Well, I'm sure your memory's better than m–

ANDY (*tensing up*). No. No – See. That's not – I don't *believe* that.

EM (*to* ANDY). Easy.

ANDY. Because *that*, I think? Is basically bullshit, okay? I think your memory is perfectly fine.

FRED. I just meant sometimes people remember things in different –

ANDY (*measured*). Nope. Nope.

EM. Andy.

ANDY. Not everything is subject to – There is such a thing as empirical reality, okay? And I know what that reality is. And what it was. And I will not sit here and allow you to tell me that what I remember, with utter clarity and and and and specificity –

FRED. I only meant –

EM. You do realize, right? You understand that when you cast *doubt* on the accuracy of a victim's story – ?

FRED. Oh, I know.

EM. – or even a single *detail* of that story, that every time you *do* that you re-expose them to the original trauma all over again. You do realize that?

FRED. I do.

EM. Which can be every bit if not more traumatizing.

FRED. I understand.

EM. So you might want to keep that in mind.

FRED (*to* EM). Excuse me one second.

The accordion door has opened again. FELIX*'s head peeks out.*

I think it's free now, Felix, if you want to – ?

FELIX *shyly emerges carrying toothbrush, toothpaste. While the sliding door is open we can see that the small room contains a twin bed – crucifix on the wall overhead – and an accumulation of neatly arranged items.* FELIX *silently makes his way toward the bathroom. Once he is gone,* ANDY *takes a deep breath, tries to continue –*

ANDY. Okay. So. This is called a reconciliation contract – ?

– but the home phone begins to ring. ANDY *gives up.*

(*Sotto, to* EM.) – okay, fuck it. This is bullshit –

EM (*overlapping*). Why are you stopping?

ANDY (*continuous, sotto*). – no, this whole – I mean, what's the *point*? It's fucking pointless and humiliating and he's not going to suddenly just – *asking for what he needs = humiliating*

EM (*sotto*). So let's do the contract.

ANDY (*sotto, continuous*). – spontaneously revise – I don't want to do it.

EM (*sotto*). Then what do you *want* to do?

ANDY (*sotto*). Let's just go.

EM (*sotto*). Is that what you *want*?

ANDY (*sotto*). Well, what do *you* want?

EM (*sotto*). I didn't want to be here in the first place.

ANDY (*sotto*). So let's go.

EM (*sotto*). As long as that's what you *want*.

ANDY (*sotto*). It is what I want. Yes it is. (*Aloud, to* FRED.) Sorry.

FRED. It's fine.

An answering machine beeps and the ringing stops as EM *and* ANDY *continue.*

EM. And you said everything you wanted to say.

ANDY. How am I supposed to answer that?

EM. Cuz now's the time, okay? Cuz we're not coming back.

ANDY. Right. Right. Yeah, I think I pretty much… um –
(*Aloud, to* FRED, *double-checking letter.*) um, just you
know, how my life has been… compromised –

FRED. Right.

ANDY. – and the pain that I feel.

FRED. You talked about that.

ANDY (*beat, reviewing his notes*). Oh – and, to tell you – um,
that you are, you know, fundamentally, um… evil. I said that,
right? → calling him "fundamentally evil" does little to make
andy feel better

EM. Yes. Earlier, you did.	ANDY. I think I said that already.	FRED. You did say that.

ANDY. Right. Okay.

EM. Time to go.

> ANDY *and* EM *gather their things, rise to go.*

FRED. I know this can't have been much fun.

EM (*tight smile*). Not a lot, no.

FRED. Maybe you'll have more fun at the water park.

> EM *freezes, turns to* ANDY, *whispers.*

EM (*sotto*). How does he know that?

ANDY (*sotto*). *I* told him that.

EM (*inaudible*). Please don't tell him *that*.

ANDY (*inaudible*). Okay.

EM (*inaudible*). There's no reason for him to know *anything*
like that.

ANDY (*inaudible*). I know that. I just –

EM (*inaudible*). *Ever*. Okay?

ANDY (*inaudible*). *Okay.* (*Full voice, to* FRED.) Anyway.

FRED. Anyway it was real nice to see you again, Andy. (*Beat.*)
I'm sorry you don't feel the same way.

EM (*evenly*). Well. We don't.

FRED. Okay.

EM. Sorry.

FRED. That's okay.

ANDY. But. I mean. But. I mean.

EM. What?

ANDY. Nothing, I just –

EM. Are we going?

ANDY. Yeah.

EM. Great.

ANDY. We're gonna go.

EM (*to* FRED). Bye.

FRED. Bye-bye.

ANDY. Bye.

> ANDY *and* EM *exit out the front door.* FRED *remains where
> he is, staring straight ahead.* FELIX *crosses from the
> bathroom into the kitchen. From outside we hear car doors
> slam, ignition, car pulling out and away.* DEE *leans in the
> kitchen doorway, seeing* FRED, *lost in thought.*

DEE. All gone?

> FRED *doesn't respond.*

Fred?

FRED. All gone.

DEE. Mmm.

FRED. They're taking their boy to the water park.

DEE. Well, I hope they have a lovely time.

FELIX *exits the kitchen, en route to his room, clutching a carton of milk, a box of breakfast cereal, plastic bowl and spoon.*

Change is on the table, Felix.

FELIX *wordlessly collects his change, enters his room and pulls the door closed behind him.*

You're welcome.

DEE *returns to kitchen.* FRED *moves the joystick on his wheelchair and travels across the room toward his electric piano. He searches through a stack of sheet music, finds what he wants, sets it up above the keyboard, then chooses a CD – peering closely without his glasses – and now inserts it into a player near the piano. Music begins – a Chopin Prelude – and* FRED *begins to play along, noiselessly, his fingers vaguely touching the keys.*

GIO *returns from his bedroom, different pants, socks in hand. Finds shoes by the front door, sits to put on shoes, socks – an ankle monitor plainly visible on his right leg.*

GIO (*over the music*). Whatzat, Fred?

FRED. Hmm?

GIO. What you're playin'?

FRED. Oh, this is by Chopin –

GIO (*pretending to know*). Ohhh, *Chopin.*

The music continues as FRED *stops playing along.*

FRED. – called the 'Raindrop' Prelude. Isn't that pretty?

GIO (*barely listening*). Yes it is.

FRED. He wrote that in a monastery on an island in the middle of the Mediterranean while he was listening to the rain falling on the roof overhead – the way that note sounds like the rain going drop drop drop?

GIO. I hear that.

FRED. Cuz ya know, he had something of a tragic life –

GIO. Who did, Chopin?

FRED. – oh, very sad –

GIO. I did not know that.

FRED. – or complicated, anyway, cuz you know, he fell in love with the wrong person, and he asked her to marry him but the family broke off the engagement and oh, he was heartbroken for the rest of his life –

GIO (*standing*). 'Scuse me, Fred.

GIO exits, as DEE enters, bringing a bag of cookies to the table.

DEE (*to* FRED). Gotcha Nutter Butters.

FRED. Hmm? (*He turns volume down on CD player.*) Oh Nutter Butters!

DEE. That's the family pack so it oughta last you but the IGA wouldn't take the EBT card so I used your cash and I'm putting your change right here.

FRED. Thank you for that.

DEE. You getcha coffee?

FRED. I had some coffee.

DEE. You getcha breakfast?

FRED. I wasn't hungry.

DEE. Gotta have something.

FRED. I had a yoghurt.

DEE. You did your number two?

FRED. Yes I did.

DEE. You empty the bag?

FRED. Oh yes.

DEE. You took your pills?

FRED (*beat*). Oh shoot.

DEE. Ah, Fred.

FRED. Shooty-shoot shoot.

DEE. I put it on the checklist.

FRED. I know that.

DEE. Didja check the checklist?

FRED. I forgot.

DEE. Gotta check the checklist.

FRED. Forget my head if it wasn't screwed on.

DEE. Can't take 'em on an empty stomach, so whatcha want, a smoothie?

FRED. Yes, please.

DEE (*heading for the kitchen*). Blueberry or banana?

FRED. Blueberry.

DEE. Blueberry.

FRED. Thank you, Dee.

DEE. When's the van comin'?

FRED. Twelve-thirty.

DEE. Better comb your hair.

> DEE *enters kitchen.* FRED *turns back toward the keyboard, turns up volume on CD player, resumes playing as the front door opens.* IVY *enters – sunglasses, shoulder bag, travel mug.*

IVY. Gentlemen.

FRED. Oh oh oh is it that time?

IVY. Shut that off, now. Let's go. (*Calling out.*) *Gio. Felix. Eleven-thirty. Circle up.*

DEE *brings* FRED's *bottled smoothie and pills from kitchen as* FRED *turns off music, steers toward the table.*

DEE (*to* IVY). Morning.

IVY. Morning.

DEE. Want some coffee?

IVY. Got my own coffee.

DEE. Ya get my voicemail?

IVY. I got your voicemail. (*Calling out.*) *Let's do it. Don't make me wait.*

GIO *enters from bedroom, crossing into kitchen.* IVY *settles in at table, takes out files, iPad.*

How ya doin', Fred?

FRED. Ohhhh, you know –

IVY. Same old same old?

FRED. – can't complain –

IVY. No news good news.

FRED. – and if ya do no one listens.

IVY. Don't I know that.

FRED. Did you and Damon make it to the lake?

IVY. Nah, couldn't do it. Damon's mom's busted her knee.

FRED (*sympathetically*). *Ohhhhhh.*

IVY. Six hours in the emergency room.

FRED. How on earth?

IVY. Well, ya know, She's eighty-three. She tripped and fell.

FRED. Oh golly.

IVY. Osteoporosis. (*Snaps fingers*.) Bones just snap right in half.

FRED. Does she take calcium?

IVY. Too late for that. Never did take care of herself. Didn't eat right. Twenty pounds overweight. Smoked two packs a day, sixty years. Falls on that knee it's like a Pringles or something.

FRED. Is she in a cast?

IVY. Walking cast. Be on crutches three months.

FRED. Well, she's lucky you were there.

IVY. Yeah, she'll be alright, but we didn't make it to the lake.

FRED. Next week.

IVY. *Gio, Felix. Let's go.*

GIO (*from kitchen door, sarcastic-formal*). Uh, I am attempting to avail myself of the coffee-maker if that's acceptable?

IVY. Getcha coffee and sit down – whatsamatter, Felix?

GIO *returns to kitchen as* FELIX*'s head sticks out of his door, holding a bowl of cereal and spoon.*

FELIX. Got my cereal.

IVY. Well, why'ntcha come eat it at the table like a normal person?

GIO (*in kitchen, to* DEE). What happened to the soymilk?

DEE (*from kitchen*). Somebody *used* all the soymilk.

GIO (*from kitchen*). Why'ntcha get some more?

DEE (*from kitchen*). Cuz nobody *asked* me to.

GIO (*from kitchen*). Cuz I didn't know we were *out of it*.

DEE (*from kitchen*). Well, you're the one that *uses* it.

GIO (*from kitchen*). And you're the one knew it was gone.

FELIX *joins* IVY *and* FRED *at the table.* FELIX *eats cereal from a plastic bowl.*

IVY. Whatcha got, Mini Wheats?

FELIX. Cinnamon Toast Crunch.

IVY. Cinnamon Toast Crunch.

GIO *enters from kitchen, sniffing coffee.*

GIO (*with distaste*). Kinda coffee's this?

FRED (*with pleasure*). French *vanilla.*

GIO....the fuck?

DEE (*to* GIO, *from kitchen*). And if you gotta problem with
that –

DEE. – maybe you oughta be making your *own* coffee sometime.	GIO. What's the matter with regular American-style coffee?

FRED (*re: coffee*). I think it's *wonderful.*

DEE *enters. All take seats around the table.*

DEE. Thank you, Fred.

(IVY.) First up –   Who is Ivy? social worker? M/F?

GIO (*muttering with disgust*). *French vanilla.*

IVY. – gotta new situation. Effective July thirty-first, County
Clerk's office has extended the perimeter to twenty-five
hundred feet –

FRED. Oh, not again. This is so silly –	DEE. You *cannot* be serious. So *half a mile* is what you're telling me.	IVY. – which is fifty percent wider than the current radius – yeah, I can do the math, Dee –	GIO. *Ah, get the fuck outta here.*

IVY (*continuous*). – if ya'd let me finish the sentence?

FRED. I just don't understand why they'd *do* that.

IVY. Cuz there was a petition, Fred. Don'tchall watch the news? Your neighbors signed a petition. That is why City Council voted to *extend* that radius –

DEE. Which means what, in practical terms?

IVY. In practical terms, it means ya can't use the bus stop on K Street, and ya can't be shopping at IGA no more.

| FRED. Well, see, now that's just not fair. – | DEE. Well honey, that puts us in a bit of a predicament. | GIO. So where're we *sposeta* shop, then? |

FRED (*continuous*). – I mean, that hardly seems fair, does it?

IVY. Fair or not, the IGA now falls within the radius.

GIO. Radius of *what*?

IVY. Radius of Bendwood.

GIO. Fuck is *Bendwood*?

IVY. Bendwood K through six special ed.

GIO. Wait wait wait wait wait.

FRED. Is that a school?

GIO. You talkin' about the *retarded* school.

IVY (*to* FRED). Learning disabilities.

GIO. Retarded school's on the other side of Fifty-five.

IVY. Yes it is, and the IGA is twenty-*four* hundred feet from that –

DEE (*raising a hand*). If I may?

IVY. – making it a potential point of unsupervised congregation.

GIO (*dismissive*). Fuck that shit.

DEE (*to* IVY). Honey. That school is clear across the *highway* from us –

IVY. We just *established* that.

DEE. – and if the new perimeter is *half* a mile, and the only way *across* the highway is a *mile and a half* in either direction –

IVY. Dee?

DEE. – then, in order for us to have contact with these theoretical endangered children they would need to go a full two and half miles *outside* that radius, then *double back* to the IGA, or make their way across six lanes of elevated *highway* – which seems beyond the ability of most school children, retarded or otherwise.

IVY. I'm just telling ya what the law says.

GIO. Ain't no *children* congregating at the IGA anyway –

FRED. He's right.

GIO. – tellya where they *are* congregatin', is the *middle*-school kids congregating at the CVS cuz the CVS is selling vape pens with no ID so maybe it's the manager of the CVS you oughta worry about.

IVY (*trying to end it*). Just buy your groceries somewhere else, aright?

DEE. Where might you suggest?

IVY. I dunno, Dee. Go to Big Lots.

GIO. Big Lots ain't got *produce*.

FRED. They have a grocery section.

GIO. Fred. That shit is substandard. Fulla pesticides. Fulla GMOs –

FRED. I bought my applesauce.

DEE (*to* IVY). You are aware the number eight bus does not go anywhere near Big Lots? Which will necessitate the use of a *taxicab* –

IVY. So buy yerself a car.

DEE. – placing an *economic* burden on top of the physical one.

IVY. Or plant a vegetable garden, I don't really give a shit. I'm just telling ya not to shop the IGA. Y'all can live on a motherfucking *cabbage* farm, all I care.

FRED. Oh, I'd like that.

DEE. You and me both.

FRED. Out in the countryside?

DEE. Overalls, calico shirts?

FRED. A little farmhouse?

DEE. Coupla straw hats?

GIO. Well, I ain't eatin' no fuckin' produce from Big Lots, nor am I making a bee-line to go fuck any *retarded* kids.

IVY. Movin' on:

GIO. I shouldn't even be *dealing* with this shit. I'm Level *One*. Y'all stick me in with a buncha Level Threes, that's *your* mistake. That's a bureaucratic oversight –

[margin note: need to distinguish oneself from the "truly" odious/undeserving]

IVY. So:

GIO. – all because the law can't seem to distinguish between a one-time offender and these hardcore pederastic motherfuckers –

IVY. Watch yer mouth.

GIO. – that's an overly broad piece of legislation.

IVY. Well, ya know what? Nobody really wants y'all livin' *anywhere*, much less in their *neighborhood*, and I can't say as I altogether blame them –

DEE. Suggestion?

IVY. – so maybe ya oughta be thankful ya gotta roof over yer head in the first place.

DEE. Why not put us on a desert *island*?

FRED. Wouldn't that be nice?

DEE. If we strike such *unspeakable terror* in the heart of the community –

FRED. Palm trees?

DEE. – let's just simplify things: Stick us on a little island offa the intercoastal waterways. Little boat so we can row across to the mainland –

FRED. A dinghy.

DEE. – a *dinghy*. Thank you, Fred.

GIO. Fine with me.

DEE. Coupla sailor suits with the little white caps –

GIO. Y'all *oughta* be banished from human society –

FRED. Ohhhh, let's not start.

GIO. – I was makin' the law, hell yes, or *castrated*, very least.

FRED. I know that you don't mean that.

GIO. Oh yes I do.

DEE. Honey, you can visit our island anytime you like –

GIO (*quietly*). Better watch it, bruh.

DEE. – just be sure'n keep your hands off my dinghy.

GIO. *You better*	FRED. Oh, gosh,	IVY. *Hey hey hey*
shut your cock-	can't we all be	*hey hey.*
sucking mouth,	nice – Oh, *stop*	
bitch –	*it,* now.	

GIO. – no – sorry, Fred. But I've *asked* him not to address me like that – Multiple times –

FRED. He was being *funny*.

GIO. – trying to taunt me with innuendo about my sexual orientation –

FRED. It was a *joke*.

GIO. – alla which may be fine and dandy with you. That's *your* prerogative. But anytime he addresses me as *honey* or *sweetie* or *babydoll* –

DEE. Or buttercup.

GIO. – I will retaliate as I see fit, and I know the word 'cocksucker' is considered pejorative, but not in reference to someone who by his own admission has sucked cocks *on a regular basis*.

IVY (*easily*). Alright, alright –

DEE (*to* GIO). Careful, baby. That's *hate speech*.

GIO. Yeah, cuz I *hate* you.   *invocation of the law for protection*

DEE (*laughing*). Oh my *goodness*.

FRED. You don't hate Dee.

DEE. Thought the Lord said *love* thy enemies.

GIO (*incredulous*). Lord never said *that*. Wherezit scripture says that? Felix, look it up. Psalms five – five: thou shalt hate the wicked and the workers of iniquity. And y'all gotta be the most iniquitous buncha motherfuckers I ever seen.

IVY. As opposed to *you*.

GIO. No no no. I made a mistake. Never denied that. And I paid my debt to society. Even Steven. Then they go and stick yer ass on the *registry*, keep ya on a public database in legal
finality   purgatory rest of yer fuckin' life –

IVY (*dismissive*). Yeah, yeah, yeah –

GIO. – that's called *double jeopardy*, aright? Shit's clearly
invocation of the law, again   unconstitutional.

IVY. So write your congressman. Now, Dee.

DEE. Yes, ma'am.

IVY. Said ya gotta problem.

DEE. Yes I do.

IVY. Let's hear it.

DEE. Though, strictly speaking, it's not an *individual* problem –

IVY (*overlapping*). Yeah yeah, spit it out.

DEE. – as much as a *collective* one. The problem being that this *area*, in which we currently find ourselves, is designated as a *common* area –

GIO (*quietly to* FELIX). Fuck's he talking about?

DEE. – and I see no legitimate reason why *some* of us cannot confine our personal belongings to our *private* space.

GIO. You talkin' 'bout my *bench*?

IVY (*re:* GIO*'s weight bench*). Talking about *that*?

FRED (*to* DEE). But Gio uses it.

IVY. What's it gotta be sitting there for?

GIO. Not botherin' nobody sitting there.

DEE. It bothers me.

GIO. It's an *inanimate object*.

DEE. It's *unsightly*.

GIO. And Fred got his little piano sitting right there don't see nobody complainin' 'bout *that*.

DEE. His piano is *tasteful*. Your shit is *distasteful*.

GIO. Yeah, Martha Stewart. Go fuck yourself.

DEE *stands, walks to where a blanket conceals an object leaning against the wall.*

DEE. And when I raised an objection, he entered *my* private
space with yonder baseball bat and proceeded to vandalize
a piece of *my* personal property –

*He pulls back the blanket to reveal the evidence: A framed
movie poster, glass broken, with a tear running down the
middle.*

– which happens to be an original 1972, first-run edition of
the lobby art for the Oscar-nominated *Lady Sings the Blues*
featuring Miss Diana Ross, with an estimated resale value of
two hundred seventy-five dollars – if you care to look on eBay
– which amount is now owed to me, in addition to the four
dollars and seventy-three cents for the produce I purchased for
him not this very morning at the IGA –

GIO. Cuz they're *green*, bruh.

DEE. – for which he has yet to reimburse me –

GIO. They're fuckin' *green*.

DEE. – Bringing the total –

GIO. Didn't want bananas for *next week*, I wanted bananas for
immediate consumption.

DEE. Bringing the total –

GIO. I'll pay you when they're *edible*.

DEE. – to two hundred seventy-nine dollars and seventy-three
cents.

IVY (*with a sigh*). The sands of the hourglass of my life are
slipping away.

DEE. And should I not receive restitution within the next
fourteen days? I'm gonna open a complaint to resolve the
matter –

FRED. This is so silly.

DEE. – so if you could provide me with the necessary
documents?

FRED (*to* GIO). Why can't you just apologize?

GIO. The choice is his, Fred. He talks to me like that? I gotta respond.

FRED. I think you're being ridiculous.

GIO. Well, that's one man's opinion.

IVY. More than one.

GIO. Judge not lest y'all be judged, aright? That's John eight-seven. Y'all go on casting stones. You'll be punished when the time comes –

DEE *is laughing*.

– laugh all ya want. Me and Felix gonna be the ones laughing in the next life, cuz y'all gonna be inna lake of everlasting fire while me and Felix are sitting at the right hand of the Lord –

DEE (*overlapping*). Oh my *goodness*.

GIO (*continuous*). – Y'all are like the Canaanites. Sodomites and blasphemers. And Felix here's gotta be one of the most depraved individuals I ever met, least he got sense enough to get himself right with the Lord, so the rest of y'all can kiss my motherfuckin' ass.

IVY *pulls a blank form from her folder, hands it to* DEE *as* GIO *continues*.

IVY. Fill that out, give it back.

GIO. For He has prepared a place in my name. Felix knows what I'm talking about. John fourteen-two: My Father's house has many rooms –

DEE. Well *this* house has *five* rooms. So why don't you and your heavenly father take your shit to *your* room?

GIO. Y'all oughta be dead *already*. Oughta been on death row cuz that's some evil disgusting shit y'all done – that's an abomination unto His sight –

FRED. Let's change the subject.

GIO. – sorry, Fred, what y'all did was *rape*. You're a *rapist*, bruh. That's *factual information*.

IVY (*to* GIO). I'm not really sure you're in best position to –

GIO. – no no no no no. That's *statutory*. That's a different ball of wax. Cuz any heterosexual man alive tells you he's not attracted to adolescent girls? That man's not being truthful, alright?

IVY (*moving on*). Anybody else?

GIO. And lest we forget, that girl falsified her records. Tellin' folks she's seventeen years old with a fake ID? Judge's sposeta take that kinda shit into account but he failed in his responsibility. And *thirdly* –

IVY (*clutching her head*). Oh my god.

GIO. – ya know where that girl is, right now? Living outta a *car*, ya understand? Impecunious little white-trash bitch living outta the back seat of a Ford Fiesta on the streets of Joliet, two kids in Pampers – not *my* kids, understand. Nothing to do with me. Stuffing her mouth fulla Tostitos courtesy of the *food stamps* taxpayers like me and Felix be subsidizing outta our own pockets –

DEE (*raised hand, to* GIO). Question?

GIO. – while *I'm* the one under motherfuckin' house arrest for alla perpetuity?

DEE. Lemme understand this: So you're a *taxpayer*?

GIO. Payroll taxes, that's right, cuz I am gainfully *employed*. Unlike *your* pathetic self, cuz I got something called *business skills*.

DEE. Honey, you are nothing but a *clown*.

GIO (*calmly*). Uh-huh.

DEE. A baggy-pants *clown*.

GIO. Keep talkin'.

DEE. Take your ass back to Ringling Brothers.

GIO. Sooner be a clown than a *parasite* suckin' off an old man's disability check –

GIO. – least I got the self-respect not to take an old man's money –	DEE (*laughing*). Oh no no, Fred. Let him talk.	FRED. Dee *helps* me, Gio. I *need* his help and I'm *happy* to pay for that.	IVY. Is this really how y'all spend your time?

GIO (*continuous*). – and twenty-six weeks from now come January fifteenth when my name's expunged from the motherfuckin' registry I am gonna be two hundred and eighty miles from here in the city of Chicago and I'll be in a financial position to buy and sell every one of y'all ten times over, so when y'all come cryin' to me like little bitches please please, Gio, won'tcha help me, please? Guess what: Ya still ain't getting no two hundred seventy-nine dollars and seventy-three cents.

Cellphone rings. Everybody looks around.

IVY. Where's that coming from?

FRED. Is that a phone?

IVY (*to* GIO). Whose phone's that?

GIO. Why's she lookin' at me?

IVY. That ain't yer landline.

IVY *rises, crosses to the sound – finds* ANDY *'s phone near the sofa, picks it up.*

Who's this belong to?

No response from anyone.

Y'all know you're not sposeta have this here. Whose izzit? (*Looking at the screen on the phone.*) Which one of y'all has got a friend named Emily? (*Beat.*) Better speak up or I'm gonna confiscate it.

FRED. You know what – I think it probably belongs to a friend of mine.

IVY. To a *friend*.

FRED. Coupla friends who were in the area.

IVY. Whaddya talking about, 'friends'?

FRED. Just someone I used to know, and his wife.

IVY. And the wife's called Emily.

FRED. Uhh – his name is Andy, and hers is Emily.

IVY. Andy and Emily.

FRED. Yes.

IVY. And what kinda friends are Andy and Emily?

FRED. Well, he works for a bank in Chicago. And I think she teaches yoga.

IVY. And they came to see *you*.

FRED. And I think one of them musta left their phone.

IVY. Mm-hm. And you wouldn't be covering up for somebody, wouldja, Fred? –

FRED. No no no.   GIO (*knowing what's
                                    coming*). Here we go.

IVY. – somebody, for example, who mighta been heard to complain on more than one occasion about how he's not allowed to have a smartphone –

GIO (*to* FRED). Yeah, pin it on Gio. He gotta be guilty of *something*.

FRED. You know, I betcha they'll come back for it.

GIO. Never mind it's the *European* male that's predisposed to criminality.

IVY (*patiently to* FRED). Where do they live?

FRED. Um – I don't know the address.

GIO. <u>Fundamental purpose of law enforcement is the regulation of the black man, Fred, didn'tcha know that?</u>

IVY (*to* FRED). And how do you plan to – ?

GIO. Next thing she'll pull out that gun and shoot me *dead*. That's standard procedure in the State of Illinois –

IVY. *Hey.* Why'ntchoo shut up?

GIO (*sotto*). [don't you] – tell *me* to shut up.

IVY (*beat, laser-like*). *What'd* you say to me?

GIO (*to* FRED, *barely audible, subdued*). She heard what I said.

IVY. You better watch that mouth, son. You talk shit to these three all you want. But before you start with me you'd best evaluate the thickness of the ice upon which you skate.

GIO (*with a snort*). She got nothing on *me*.

IVY. Try me and find out.

GIO. Whadda you got?

IVY. Gotcha goin' outta your inclusion zone.

GIO. When?

IVY. *Twice.* Gotcha goin' offa GPS. Wanna see the printout?

GIO *hoists his leg up onto the table, pulls back his pants leg to show ankle monitor.*

GIO. Yeah, cuz this shit's *busted*. That's why I'm offa GPS, cuz there's a problem with the unit. Needa upgrade the system.

IVY. Top of that, GPS clocked you doing seventy-three in a forty-five-mile-an-hour zone –

GIO (*overlapping*). Wasn't me *driving*. That's a *carpool*.

IVY (*continuous*). – and I could write you up – I don't give a shit who's *driving* the car. You were *in* it, and that makes you

[handwritten margin note: is Ivy a probation officer?]

accessory and I could haul you in for *that*, I was in a bad mood.

GIO. Uh-huh. Talk to Dixon and Johnston Attorneys at Law.

IVY. No, I'm talking to you.

GIO. She got till January fifteenth. After that she got no more jurisdiction over me, cuz I'm *out*.

[handwritten margin note: threats begin (Ivy was chiller before, has clear familiarity w them)]

IVY. And until that time you are playing with a full count, and all I need is one more strike to send you back to work-release, and you'll be picking up trash on the side of the freeway the rest of your natural life. Cuz you know all about trash, don'tcha?

GIO (*calmly to* FRED). That's verbal abuse.

IVY. You heard me.

GIO. I'll notify the PB – *[handwritten note: parole board?]*

IVY (*unimpressed*). You do that.

[handwritten note: belief that the law can give him remedy]

GIO. – I'll tie her ass up in litigation next fifteen years.

IVY (*fierce*). You go right ahead you stupid piece o' shit. But I tellya what: You keep mouthing off you're gonna find out the limit of your rights real quick, ya hear me? (*Beat.*) Best pick someone else, son, cuz I ain't the one, alright?

FRED (*looking at watch*). Um. You know, I have physical therapy at twelve-thirty?

IVY. We're done. Fred, tell your friends to come get their phone.

FRED. Yes, ma'am.

DEE, FELIX *and* GIO *stand.*

IVY. Felix, you stay a second.

Outside, a car horn. FELIX *sits again.* DEE *exits into kitchen.* GIO *goes on babbling as* IVY *pulls out files, prepares to talk with* FELIX.

GIO. See, Fred, we got two standards of justice, this country.

FRED (*sympathetically*). Oh, I *know*.

GIO (*to* FRED). 'Member Ty Freeman? Friend of mine? Useta work at the Best Buy?

FRED. Ummm – ?

GIO. Any rate. Ty Freeman's Level One. Statutory bullshit, same as me. And he's walking down the street coming home from stocking shelves at the Best Buy, this is 'bout ten, twelve weeks ago, walkin' home 'round 6 p.m. minding his business, drinkin' a Arizona Iced Tea, and he's halfway home, naturally he gotta relieve himself cuz that's a twenty-three-ounce can, right? So he goes across the parking lot, alongside Panera Bread, ducks behind a minivan for modesty's sake, standing there takin' a piss, some vigilante motherfucker sees him with his dick out, calls nine-one-one he's back in Menard three more years. All for takin' a *piss*.

[handwritten: public urination is a sex offense]

FRED. Don't they have a bathroom?

GIO. The bathroom ain't the point, Fred. The point's the double-*standard* –

Doorbell rings. FRED *begins wheeling toward bedroom.* GIO *heads for the door.*

– cuz think about this. If I was a *white woman* sitting in a Starbucks or somethin' with a *baby* on my lap? I'm perfectly free to pull out my titty right there, broad daylight have my baby suckin' on *that* all day long, and you're telling me I can't even pull out my *dick* to take a *piss*?

DEE (*from kitchen door*). Maybe if your dick had some *nutritional value*…?

The doorbell rings insistently. GIO *opens the door.* EFFIE *stands there.*

EFFIE. *What is your problem?*

EFFIE (*continuous*). *I've been sitting there like fifteen minutes with the car running and my battery is about to die and I have to pee, and if I lose the hour? You owe me eleven dollars.*

GIO. Will you settle your ass down? You've been waiting fifteen *seconds*. No one's gonna be *late* –

GIO (*continuous*). – You just pulled up, girl. Take a Klonopin and relax.

GIO *exits up hallway.*

IVY (*to* GIO, *suspicious, as he goes*). Who's this?

GIO (*as he exits*). That's my ride.

IVY. Your ride.

GIO. My carpool.

EFFIE (*nearly a shriek*). *Hurry up!!!!*

EFFIE *turns to go.*

IVY. Young lady?

EFFIE *stops, stares at* IVY.

How are you this morning?

EFFIE. Fine.

IVY. May I see some identification please?

EFFIE (*beat*). Why?

IVY. May I see some ID please?

EFFIE. What for?

IVY. May I see some ID?

EFFIE. Am I being detained?

→ What kind of legal consciousness is this?

IVY. May I see some ID?

EFFIE. Am I being detained?

IVY. May I see some ID?

EFFIE. Am I being detained?

IVY. ID please?

EFFIE. Okay, but am I being detained? Cuz according to the Sixth Amendment if I'm not being legally detained –

IVY. Oh Christ Almighty.

EFFIE (*continuous*). – then I'm not required to show you an ID so I'm just asking if I'm being detained and on what charge because otherwise I do not consent to answer your questions.

IVY. I'm Officer Delgado. What's your name?

EFFIE. I do not consent to the question.

IVY. You the one likes to drive seventy miles an hour in a forty-five zone?

EFFIE (*long beat*). Am I being detained?

GIO *returns, tucking a red polo shirt with a STAPLES insignia into his khakis, heading for the door.*

GIO. Let's do it.

IVY. Young lady – ?

EFFIE. Thank you officer have an awesome day. amazing

GIO *and* EFFIE *exit, closing the door.* IVY *shakes her head, pulls out a digital recorder and power cord.*

FELIX. You wanna talk to me?

IVY. Yeah, gimme a second.

IVY *rises to plug power cord into wall.* DEE *enters from kitchen in an apron, approaches* FELIX.

DEE (*re: cereal bowl*). All done with that?

FELIX *surrenders his bowl and spoon to* DEE, *who exits back into kitchen.* IVY *positions recorder on table, sits again.*

IVY. So, if ya don't mind, I'm gonna record this conversation, long as that's alright with you?

FELIX (*surprised, innocent shrug*). Whatever.

IVY. No objection to that?

FELIX. Don't matter to me.

IVY. Alright. (*Switches it on.*) There we go. Now then: Wanna tell me about it?

FELIX (*beat*). 'Bout what?

IVY (*smiles*). Felix.

FELIX. Tell you 'bout what?

IVY. C'mon, Felix.

FELIX. Whattayou want me to tell you about?

IVY. Don't make me haveta ask.

FELIX (*confused, laughs*). I mean, maybe if you *tell* me what you want me to tell you about I could *tell* you about it but I can't *tell* you about it if you don't tell me what you want me to *tell* you about –

IVY. Felix –

FELIX. – I don't got ESP.

IVY (*with a sigh*). Alright then. Where'd ya go Tuesday morning?

FELIX (*what a bizarre question*). Tuesday *night* I went to work.

IVY. Yeah, we're talking about the *morning*.

FELIX (*shrugs*). Came home from workin' Monday night.

IVY. And you didn't go nowhere else?

FELIX. I dunno.

IVY. You don't *remember*?

FELIX (*clarifying*). *Last* Tuesday?

IVY. What time you get to work Monday night?

FELIX. Uhh. Nine-thirty.

IVY. Get to the garage nine-thirty. Watch over the cars till morning, what time you finish up?

FELIX. Seven-thirty.

IVY. 7 30 a.m. Punch out. Go to yer counselor. Ya went off your medication, innat right? —race or something else in the dialect?

FELIX. The MPA, yeah.

IVY. How long ya been off that now?

FELIX. Six months.

IVY. Six months no problems.

FELIX. No problems.

IVY. Counselor says you're doin' alright without it.

FELIX. I'm doin' pretty good.

IVY. Okay, so whatcha do after that?

FELIX. After the counselor? (*Shrugs.*) Get on the bus. Come home.

IVY. Mm-hm. Well, now let's think about that.

FELIX. Come home, go to my room, go to sleep. Same as always.

IVY. Uh-huh. Well, let's just stop and think about that for half a second see if ya might maybe wanna reconsider that answer.

Pause. FELIX *thinks.*

FELIX. Ohhh *Tuesday.*

IVY. Tuesday morning.

FELIX. *After* the counselor.

IVY. Said it three times now. Tuesday morning *after* the counselor.

FELIX (*searching his memory*)....uhhh...

IVY. You don't *remember*?

FELIX. It's like a *week* ago.

IVY. Four days.

FELIX (*guessing*). Maybe get a McMuffin?

IVY. You don't remember goin' to the library?

FELIX (*genuinely puzzled*). Nope.

IVY. You telling me you *didn't* go to the library?

FELIX. Said I don't *remember*.

IVY. Well, I'm trying to jog your memory.

FELIX (*beat*). I mean, I *been* to the library.

IVY. I *know* ya have. And we talked about that, didn't we? But you didn't go there Tuesday morning?

FELIX. I told you, I don't re–

IVY. You didn't go to the library, go on the internet?

FELIX (*how ridiculous*). No.

IVY. You're sure about that.

FELIX. Yeah.

IVY. So why's GPS say I got you in that vicinity?

Long beat, FELIX *thinks.*

FELIX. Wait – *after* the counselor?

IVY. How many times you want me to say it?

FELIX. Oh oh oh yeah to the *library*, yeah. But for just like, a second.

IVY (*disappointed*). *Felix.*

FELIX. Just for like half a minute. Like real quick in and out.

IVY. *This is what we talked about.*

FELIX. I know I but I had to check out some books.

IVY (*beat, dubious*). You were checkin' out books.

FELIX. Yeah.

IVY. Alright. So where the books at?

Pause.

It don't pay to lie to me, Felix.

FELIX. I took 'em back.

IVY. Well, that was fast.

FELIX. Put 'em in the overnight slot.

IVY. Whattaya, like a speed-reader?

FELIX. I didn't like 'em so I took 'em back.

IVY. What kinda books?

FELIX. Um. One about bridge.

IVY. Bridge, the card game.

FELIX. How to play bridge, yeah.

IVY. Who ya playin' bridge with?

FELIX. Gio plays bridge so I was gonna learn. So we can play.

IVY. And what else?

FELIX. What else what.

IVY. Ya said books, *plural*.

FELIX. Uh – Stephen King.

IVY. Which one?

FELIX. *The Stand*.

IVY. That's a long book.

FELIX. *Too* long, yeah. That's why I took it back.

IVY. And you didn't go online when you were there.

FELIX (*simply*). Nope.

Long pause. They stare at each other.

IVY. You know they got records of that.

FELIX. Okay, yeah maybe for a minute, but –

IVY (*disappointed*). *Felix.*

FELIX. – I *had* to. I *had* to – I didn't have a choice.

IVY. Fuckzat mean ya *had* to?

FELIX. I can't be looking at nothing at the *library*. They got filters all the computers. They're blocked. I can't look at nothing I'm not s'pose to. I stay in the adult section, the whole time I'm there. I don't go nowhere I shouldn't –

IVY. So what the hell you going online for?

FELIX. To buy a ticket.

IVY. …*lottery* ticket?

FELIX. Plane ticket.

IVY (*dubious laugh*). A *plane* ticket?

FELIX. Yeah.

IVY. Where ya plannin' on goin'?

FELIX. See my sister.

IVY (*eyebrows raised*). In *San Antonio*?

FELIX. And Southwest is the cheapest and they got a discount. It's fifty dollars cheaper if you do it online –

IVY (*amazed laugh*). *Felix?*

FELIX. – and I don't got fifty dollars to just throw away but you can't get the discount unless you go online to Southwest.

IVY. No no no no no. Felix. You can't go to *Texas*.

FELIX. That's not true.

IVY. Are you outta your mind?

FELIX. No. I can't go to *Harris County* –

IVY. You can't even leave the *state* without talking to *me* first –

FELIX. Call the judge. Ask him yourself.

IVY. – now, if you'd come and *talked* to me, maybe I could getcha an exception, *maybe*, but ya can't come telling me this *after* ya already went and bought the ticket –

FELIX (*overlapping*). This is the first time I *see* you!

IVY (*continuous*). – or didja figure you'd sneak off in the middle of the night and nobody'd notice you're gone?

FELIX. Why don't you look at what the judge said, huh? Go look it up. You always accuse me of doing something wrong, you know? Always suspicious of me. What do I ever do? I go to work. I park the cars. In the morning, I come home. Go to my room. Lock the door. Put in my earplugs. I don't talk to nobody. Mind my business. Study my Bible. *That's all I ever do*. That's it. So why's everybody gotta be looking at me like I'm some kinda liar, huh?

IVY. Well, maybe cuz you gotta history of lyin' to people.

FELIX *goes silent, shakes his head.*

Better get your money back on that plane ticket.

FELIX. It's non-refundable.

IVY. Or get your sister to come here instead.

FELIX. She can't come here.

IVY. Why can't she?

FELIX (*beat*). She got cancer.

FELIX *holds back tears.*

IVY. Sorry to hear that.

FELIX. Yeah.

IVY. That's too bad.

FELIX. Stage three.

IVY. She doin' chemo?

FELIX *nods*

Well, that can't be fun.

FELIX. I pray for her every day, you know? Every day I ask Him to help her. Every single day.

IVY. Couldn't hurt.

FELIX. Why can't he take *me*, you know? Wanna punish *me* go ahead, I don't care but why punish *her*? She didn't do nothing. She's like the only person left in the world that don't hate me so why's he gotta take her away? I pray every single – He don't even care. Why's He gotta take away from me the one person I got left in the whole world –

FELIX *is overcome with tears.*

IVY (*gently*). Hey.

FELIX. – I don't got no one else. Why's he gotta take it out on her?

IVY. Getcher self a Kleenex.

FELIX *goes to kitchen, comes back with paper towel, wiping his eyes.*

Ya alright?

FELIX *nods, sits.*

Aright. Now. Let's s'pose for the sake of argument I was to call up your sister and say what *kind* of cancer you got –

FELIX. Call her right now.

IVY. – cuz I'm sure there's an *element* of truth to what you're saying –

FELIX. Gimme your phone. I'll dial it for you. You can talk to her right now.

IVY. Breast cancer? Lung cancer?

FELIX. Colon cancer.

IVY. Colon cancer.

FELIX *nods*.

Well, that's not good.

FELIX. Only thing I want is to see her before it's too late, you know? Only one thing. But you sit here. And all you say is no, no, no –

IVY. Felix –

FELIX. – like I don't know what the rules are. Like I'm the only one ever messes up. Gio goes outside the zone, misses curfew. You don't say nothing. Dee talks back to you. Uses curse words –

IVY. Felix:

FELIX. – whyzit I'm the only one?

IVY. Listen to me. I got forty-seven clients, aright? Forty-seven of y'all I gotta deal with on a weekly basis all shapes and sizes but ya all got one thing in common, okay? Every one of you's a *victim*. Everybody's misunderstood, been done wrong, system's broke, system ain't fair blah blah, and that may or may not be the case – but I'll tell ya something. If y'all feel so *victimized*? Maybe that gives ya a little idea how ya made *other* people feel, okay? (*Beat.*) Now. I'm not saying that you're *definitely lying* to me, Felix? –

FELIX. *I didn't do nothing. Why don't you listen?*

IVY (*continuous*). – But it's not hard for me to find out – Okay: First off, you're not sposeta be anywhere *near* the *library*. And you *know* that. That's a big strike-one right there. But I'm a generous person. Might even letcha slide on that one cuzza yer sister and all. But lemme tell ya what. If I email that library right now and ask for those records, and *then* find out you been lying to me –

FELIX. *You never listen to anything I say.*

IVY. – and *especially* if I find out you been going on *Facebook* again?

FELIX *goes still.*

If you been tryin' to contact your daughter on Facebook? Cuz if I *do* find that out, and I *will* find it out, Felix –

FELIX *(quietly to himself).* Tu no sabes nada de mi.

IVY. – if I *do* find it out? That's a re-offense. And then we gotta go back to the judge. And if you *lie* to me about it? That looks even worse.

FELIX *is rigid, controlled. We briefly notice* DEE, *in the kitchen, just within earshot.*

I don't care what you think

FELIX *(to himself).* A mi no importe lo que tu piensas. Yo adoro a m'hija –

IVY *(overlapping).* English, Felix. We're on record now.

FELIX *(continuous, defiant).* – di lo que tu quieres de mi – *I said I love my daughter*, okay?

IVY. Well, ya gotta funny way of showin' it.

FELIX. I don't care what you think. God knows the truth. He knows I love her.

IVY. Yeah, well, my husband loves his Golden Retriever he didn't stick his dick in her mouth.

FELIX *goes silent, slowly shakes his head.*

How old's she now? Thirteen? Fourteen? Sounds about right. *(Beat.)*

And you're telling me you didn't go online at any point and try and make contact?

FELIX *is immobile, silent.*

Alright. Tell you what. You can either tell me now. Make both our lives easier. And I'll go to bat for you with the judge. Do my best, try and see you don't go back. Or least send ya to Rushville, getcha back in rehab. And *maybe* –

FELIX (*quietly*). I'm not going to Rushville.

IVY (*continuous*). – listen to me – *maybe* we can even find a
way for you to see your sister, aright? So that's option
number one.

FELIX. I'm not going back.

IVY. *Or* you *could* make me spend the rest of my day getting a
warrant, chasing down those records and frankly I got better
things to do with my afternoon. So that's option two, and if
that's your choice, Felix, well, in that case I can't help ya out
with the judge, but –

FELIX (*to himself, calmly*). No me importa lo que piensa. No
voy allí. You got nothing and I'm not going.

IVY. – can I finish, okay? Can I do that? Cuz there's a third
option –

IVY *reaches into her bag and pulls out a portable polygraph
and begins to hook it up to her iPad.*

– if ya gimme a chance, alright? Cuz if you work *with* me,
not *against* me, that's gonna count for something. Like say,
for example, if you'd be willing to take a polygraph right
here and now, demonstrate you're being cooperative, that'd
go a long way to convince a judge of your sincerity. And
long as you don't got any reason *not* to wanna take it – ? See
what I'm saying?

Silence. FELIX *stares at the polygraph.*

Ya think ya'd be up for that?   FORESHADOWING

DEE (*unseen, from kitchen*). Don't do it, Felix.

IVY. *Dee?* Nobody's talking to you.

DEE *appears in kitchen door.*

| DEE. Polygraph's *bullshit* anyway and she knows that. She's just trying to manipulate you into false confession – | IVY. Dee. Keep yerself out of it. Not sposeta be eavesdropping on people's private conver– |

(Handwritten margin note: She's not really advocate. Playing both good/bad cop)

IVY. – *Hey!* Why'ntcha go take a walk or something, get yerself some fresh air?

DEE. Because this is *my* home, darl–

IVY. This ain't *your home*. This property belongs to the Lutheran Social Service of Illinois and you oughta be extremely grateful your neighbors haven't burned it to the ground with y'all sleeping inside.

DEE (*to* FELIX). Say I request counsel.

FELIX. I request counsel.

IVY. Felix. Look at me. Dee is not your friend in this situation.

FELIX. You're not my friend.

IVY. That's right. I'm your PO. But I can help you. And Dee can't.

DEE. Request counsel.

IVY. *God damn it, Dee* –

| DEE. He is exercising his constitutional right against self-incrimi– write me up for *what*? | IVY (*continuous*). *– you better back your ass outa here 'less you want me to write you up, cuz you are –* | FELIX. I request counsel. |

IVY (*continuous*). – Thirty-one section A: Anyone who knowingly obstructs the performance of a peace officer commits a Class-A misdemeanor and I don't think you're exactly in a position to be doing that, are ya?

DEE (*calmly, to* FELIX). A polygraph is inadmissible in the State of Illinois –

IVY. Dee? Last chance.

DEE (*continuous*). – *unless you agree to it*, and all it measures is how much you don't want to take it.

IVY. But if Felix is telling the truth then he don't got any *reason* not to wanna take it. Isn't that right, Felix?

FELIX. I request counsel.

Outside, a different car horn sounds.

DEE (*calls out*). Fred? Van's here.

They wait for FRED. *Long pause. When he doesn't appear:*

IVY. Felix, if you decline that's gonna make you non-compliant –

DEE (*to* FELIX). That's not non-compliant, that's *delayed* compliance –

IVY. – That's it. I'm writing you up. You're in some serious shit, my friend –

FELIX (*losing his shit at* DEE). *Just shut up!! Why'ntchoo ever shut up, huh? Alla you!! You're not my friends and I don't want your help. So why'ntchoo shut up and leave me alone??!!!*

DEE. My *goodness*.

FELIX. I'm not *like* you, okay? And I don't like people like you. I don't like any the way you *live* and the way you *think* and the things you *do* and the things you *say* and *I don't want your help anymore*. I got all the help I need so *why'ntchoo shut up and leave me alone?*

DEE *surrenders, respectfully withdrawing.*

IVY. Felix –

FELIX (*quietly*). I request counsel.

A door opens in the hall and we hear FRED's *voice.*

FRED (*from off*). Was that the van?

DEE. They're waiting for you.

FRED (*from off*). Oh golly.

Everyone waits for FRED *to roll down the hallway, oblivious to the tension in the room.*

[handwritten margin notes:]
felix rejects dee's help
relation b/w client + att'y

dee is the jailhouse lawyer
value in longstanding experience in the system

dee is also most resentful distrustful of authority

Oh, ya know I had my little headphones on and I didn't even hear. I hope they haven't been waiting too long.

DEE. Just drove up.

FRED. Oh my gosh. Look at that. It's clouding up, isn't it? Wonder if I'm gonna need an umbrella – ?

DEE. Why'ntcha take one just in case.

FRED *looks around for an umbrella. The car horn honks again.*

FRED. Oh shoot –

DEE (*with a sigh*). Go on out. I'll bring it to ya.

DEE *turns, exits toward* FRED*'s room.*

FRED. – thank you, Dee. (*Explaining to* IVY.) It's just sometimes we have to wait out on the sidewalk and there's no cover when it starts to rain –

IVY. Mm-hmm.

FRED (*to* IVY). Good to see you, my dear. Hope you can make it to the lake this week.

IVY. Thank you, Fred.

FRED *wheels his chair to the door, opens it without too much difficulty, exits.* IVY *and* FELIX *sit in silence for a few seconds.*

Felix –?

FELIX. I request counsel.

DEE *returns with umbrella, exits out front door. More silence, then:*

IVY (*beat*). Look: You don't wanna take the polygraph, that's your business – but can I at least askya one question – ?

FELIX (*with finality*). I said all I'm gonna say. Said everything I'm gonna say, and I'm not talking no more without a lawyer. Nope. That's it. That's all.

IVY (*sadly*). Well. That's your right. You're entitled to that. But
  – I gotta be straight with ya, Felix: I *already* got the records
  from the library. (*Beat, slowly.*) So. I know what you did.
  And I was just tryin' to give you a chance to help yourself,
  come clean with me, but... you didn't wanna do that. So
  that's where we stand.   ə lie?

FELIX *is stunned, stricken.*

So, how 'bout I give ya a day to getcha stuff sorted out. You
sposeta be workin' tonight?

He shakes his head.

So whaddya say I stop by tomorrow morning, first thing,
pick ya up – ?

He shrugs.

Ye're not gonna try and run on me, are ya? Cuz ya know I'll
find ya. The minute you try and cut that monitor on your leg
I'm gonna know. So I hope you're not lying to me. The lying
just makes it worse.

He shakes his head again.

So how 'bout we say tomorrow morning, eight-fifteen?
You'll be ready to go?

FELIX *nods, then breaks down crying. His body shakes with
sobs.*

(*Slowly, sadly.*) C'mon, Felix. C'mon, you'll be alright.
(*Beat.*) And how ya think it makes *me* feel to be the one?
Why'd you gotta put me in that position? I mean, godammit
Felix, how'd you think I wasn't gonna find out?

FELIX (*through sobs*). It's her fifteenth birthday. She just
turned fifteen.

FELIX *covers his face, softly prays.*

(*Almost inaudible.*) – señor mío, Jesucristo, Dios y Hombre
verdadero, Creador, Padre y Redentor mío...

IVY. Look. I dunno. Maybe the judge'll let ya plead out. It could happen. And I'll do what I can, but… Ya gotta understand, you didn't do yourself any fav–

FELIX *abruptly stands, crosses to his room, slides door shut. Quiet.* IVY *sits for a moment, blank, rubs her eyes, takes a cookie from the package on the table, nibbles.* DEE *returns, collecting* FRED's *coffee mug.*

I'm eating one of your Nutter Butters.

DEE. Well, technically those are Fred's but I won't tell if you don't.

IVY *sighs, slowly closes her case file, iPad.*

(*From kitchen.*) Want some more coffee?

IVY. What I want is a Key Lime Martini from Outback Steakhouse but I gotta wait till five o'clock.

DEE. Anybody ever gonna do something about that window?

DEE *exits to kitchen.*

IVY. Y'all gotta Yellow Pages.

DEE. I believe if you consult the residence agreement, you'll find it's not our responsibility to provide maintenance for the property which, you've so rightly pointed out is not ours to begin with –

IVY (*deep sigh*). Yeah, well I got stuff to do so y'all getcher own window fixed.

DEE *returns with his coffee, sits with* IVY.

DEE. I think you got the job-related stress.

IVY. Yeah, that's what happens when ya gotta *job*.

DEE. Well, you know, the job market is somewhat limited for the elderly black homosexual ex-convict.

DEE *leans in, attempts to speak privately.*

(*Sotto.*) Felix going away?

IVY (*sotto*). I'm not talking about it with you.

DEE (*sotto*). Alright.

IVY (*sotto*). And maybe you oughta try not sticking your nose in other people's business.

DEE (*sotto*). I'm not sticking any *part* of my anatomy where it's not supposed to be.

IVY (*rubs her eyes, checks watch*). How can I be so tired?

DEE. Oh, it *must* be exhausting keeping track of all these penises.

IVY (*standing*). I'm out.

> IVY *unplugs her power cords, etc., returning everything to her shoulder bag.*

DEE. I get a little tired myself, you know. Being told where to buy my groceries. Which streets I'm allowed to walk down. What time of day I gotta be indoors –

IVY. Whaddya want me to tellya, Dee? You know the law. You don't like the situation you're in, whose fault is that?

DEE. Yes, ma'am.

IVY. People do what they gotta do to protect their *family*, alright? That's just common sense. Same as you'd do to protect your *own* family.

DEE. You've obviously never met my family.

> IVY *zips up her shoulder bag.*

I get tired of people calling me evil, calling me crazy, telling me I'd be better off dead, telling me who I'm not allowed to love –

IVY. Ah, cut that shit out. Now you're gonna piss me off –

DEE. My *good*ness.

IVY. – *You didn't love that boy.* What's the matter with you? You're *sexually attracted to children.*

DEE. *One* child.

IVY. That's. Not. Love. All right? You don't get to use that word. It's a *sickness*. That's all it is. Love's got nothing to *do* with it. If you loved that boy you never woulda done what you did.

DEE (*noncommittal*). Well, let's agree to disagree.

DEE *sips his coffee.* IVY *finishes packing up her stuff.*

[margin handwriting: rhetoric in Allen similar]

IVY. And I know y'all got the short straw. And I'm sorry about that, cuz y'all are fucked for life, and you're never gonna change and that's a cross y'all gotta bear cuz nobody ever asked to be born that way but that don't change the simple fact that *some* things are just right and wrong. And you know that as well as I do.

[margin handwriting: impossibility of rehab. pathology, public health]

DEE. Here's an interesting fact: Did you know this? There is a tribe of people living right now as we speak, up in the mountains of New Guinea – I'm not making this up – and in *that* community, see, they believe that, in order for a boy to become a man, they got this little ritual in which alla the boys, starting around age seven or eight, they teach 'em how to perform fellatio on the older men of the tribe –

IVY *turns to leave, disgusted.*

IVY. I'm not listening to this –

DEE. – It's *true*, honey – and then they gotta swallow the semen –

IVY. Aw, *shut up. Shut up. Just shut the fuck up.* (*Nauseated.*) *Aw god* –

DEE. – it's anthropology, baby.

IVY (*light-headed with disgust*). – *the fuck is wrong with you?* (*Harsh.*) Don't ever say shit like that to your PO. You don't wanna go to counseling no more, that's up to you. But do yourself a favor, don't go around *sayin'* shit like that.

DEE. Yes, ma'am.

IVY. Whyd'ya think you never got early release? Whyd'ya think you did the full fifteen while Gio's out in three and a half?

It's cuz you go around saying shit like that, makin' yerself
sound crazy, and I don't think you're crazy but *fuck*, Dee –
you don't even sound like you're *ashamed*. And if you're not
ashamed? For fuck's sake at least try and *pretend* like you are.

IVY *crosses, opens the front door.*

You didn't love that boy, Dee. I don't care what you think.
And that boy didn't love you, neither. Maybe your *mother*
loved you, I dunno, but not that boy. You know that,
don'tcha?   role of POW
                                             counselor, etc.

DEE. Well, you'd have to ask him that.

IVY. Well, that's not possible, is it?

DEE *says nothing.* IVY *exits out the front door.* DEE *sips his*
coffee. We hear a car start up and pull away. After a
moment, almost inaudibly, we hear FELIX*'s voice coming*
from his room:

FELIX. Padre nuestro,
    Que estás en el cielo.
    Santificado sea tu nombre.
    Venga tu reino.
    Hágase tu voluntad en la tierra como en el cielo.
    Danos hoy nuestro pan de cada día.
    Perdona nuestras ofensas,
    como también nosotros perdonamos a los que nos ofenden –

last time we see felix in the play. text + his role to be forgotten/
marginalized – making him forgettable + british – american audience
via spanish

DEE *stands, crosses to the CD player.*

No nos dejes caer en tentación y líbranos del mal. Amén.

DEE, *waits, listens, thinks* FELIX *has stopped. Then:*

Señor mío, Jesucristo, Dios y hombre verdadero, Creador,
Padre, Redentor mío, por ser vos quien sois, bondad infinita
y por que os amo sobre todas las cosas –

DEE *chooses a CD from a stack, puts it in the player, presses*
play: A Diana Ross single begins to play, as FELIX
continues to pray.

You can punish me with the fires of hell...

– me pesa de todo corazón haberos ofendido, también me
pesa porque podéis castigarme con las penas del infierno.
Animado con tu divina gracia, propongo firmemente…

DEE *turns up the volume, drowning out* FELIX, *exits as the music swells. Lights out.*

End of Act One.

melding
the relevant
images

the longer Felix has been dead, the more culpable the audience for forgetting him

ACT TWO

9 p.m. Same day. Dark outside. Lamps on, dimly illuminating the room.

DEE *at the table with a glossy magazine, herbal tea.* ANDY *seated as far from* DEE *as possible, envelope at his side, watching a game streaming on his phone. The phone charger is plugged into a wall outlet. We can hear the tinny play-by-play. After some time:*

DEE. Did you enjoy the water park?

> *After a long moment,* ANDY *realizes he's the one being addressed.*

ANDY. Did I what?

DEE. The water park.

ANDY. What about it?

DEE. Or didn't you go?

ANDY (*suspicious*)....when?

DEE. Weren't you planning on going to the water park?

ANDY. We *went* to the water park.

DEE. Well, that's why I asked.

ANDY. *What* did you ask?

DEE. If you enjoyed yourself.

ANDY. Oh. Um. Got rained out.

DEE. Aww.

ANDY. About ten minutes after we got there.

DEE. That's a shame.

DEE *sips his tea.* ANDY *nods, watches his game for a long time, then:*

ANDY. Did I *tell you* we were going to the water park?

DEE. You told Fred. Fred told me.

ANDY. Oh right. (*Beat.*) Splash Valley, it's called. It's for kids, ya know.

DEE. And why is *rain* a problem at a *water* park?

ANDY. Well, you know –

DEE. – Oh *lightning*.

ANDY. – *Lightning*. Blew the whistle. Everybody out.

DEE. Don't want your kids to get electrocuted.

ANDY. But they had arcade games and stuff, so. I dunno. He had fun.

DEE. Well, that's wonderful.

ANDY. Anyway.

DEE. And I do apologize for the smell.

ANDY (*beat*). For the – ?

DEE. You don't smell that?

ANDY. Oh. Um – ?

DEE. Or am I being overly sensitive?

ANDY. – I guess – possibly – ?

DEE (*with disgust*). Hmm-*mm*.

ANDY. – now that you mention it – ?

DEE. Started thinking it was *me*.

ANDY. – kinda rank.

DEE. Cuz I will not tolerate a nasty smell.

ANDY. No, I agree.

DEE. I was fastidious as a child. My mother – she was a smoker and I used to complain about the smell coming from her ashtrays and she'd say why'nt you mind your own goddamn business. (*Beat.*) But then she died of emphysema so I guess she learned her lesson.

ANDY. Right.

DEE. So I do apologize.

ANDY. Really not all that noticeable. ↗ the smell is felix

The home phone begins to ring, once, twice, three times – ANDY *turns, looks.* DEE *ignores it, sips his tea. Another half a ring and it stops, beeps.*

DEE. You're sure there's nothing I can offer you?

ANDY (*declining*). Thanks.

DEE. Other than alcohol.

ANDY. I'm fine.

DEE. We're not permitted alcoholic beverages. (*Beat.*) There was a time in my life when I always used to have a little something before bedtime. In my carefree younger days. (*Beat.*) Mais, où sont les neiges d'antan?

ANDY (*no idea what he's talking about*). Right.

DEE. I took six years of French in school.

ANDY. Uh-huh.

DEE. – but I find little practical application in my daily life.

ANDY (*not wanting to talk*). Um. What time does Fred generally – [return]?

DEE. Shoulda been here by now. He's normally home by nine. (*Beat.*) Neuf heures du soir.

ANDY. What's he do, like telemarketing?

DEE. Telephone sales.

ANDY. Right.

DEE (*proffering mug*). We do have chamomile tea?

ANDY (*declining*). Thanks.

DEE. Or Lemon Zinger. (*Beat.*) Or Red Zinger. (*Beat.*) Cranberry Apple Zinger.

ANDY. Not for me.

DEE. Is that a sporting event you're watching?

ANDY. This? Yeah.

DEE. You're free to watch our television.

ANDY.... whaddayou guys got, dish?

DEE. It's not on broadcast television?

ANDY (*slightly surprised*). No. Well, you can stream it on – oh –

DEE. We're not allowed access to the internet.

ANDY. Right. Or if you have the app for your –

DEE. We're not allowed to have smartphones.

ANDY. – right. (*Beat.*) Anyway. Orioles/White Sox.

DEE. And which of the opposing teams is winning?

ANDY. Sox by two.

DEE. Well, good for them.

ANDY. You a Sox fan?

DEE. No.

ANDY. Baseball fan?

DEE. That I am not. We do have a DVD player.

ANDY. Okay.

DEE. I have over three hundred classic films on Blu-ray and DVD.

ANDY. Old-school.

DEE. Including the entire body of cinematic work of both Miss Diana Ross and the late Whitney Houston.

ANDY. Cool.

DEE (*beat*). And you *really don't* smell that?

ANDY. Yeah, now I do.

DEE. Oh *honey*.

ANDY. Definitely something.

DEE (*with disgust*). Hmm-*mm*.

ANDY. Mold, maybe?

DEE. That's not mold.

DEE *stands, exits down the hallway.*

ANDY. Or – Sometimes – we had a thing, when I was little – when I was little we had a crawl space under the house and sometimes animals – squirrel I guess, maybe – would get up inside there and – I dunno. Couldn't find their way back out or something.

DEE *has returned with an oscillating fan connected to a long extension cord. He places it near the door, switches it on, opens front door, allowing the breeze in.*

Maybe crack that window? (*Re: broken window.*) What's up with your window?

DEE. This window? (*Matter of fact.*) That was done with a shotgun.

ANDY (*beat*). What do you mean, like a – ? Like –

DEE. Like a shotgun.

ANDY. – like, as a threat?

DEE. I don't think it was a gesture of goodwill.

ANDY. Wow. And did they ever… find the person – ?

DEE. I'm not sure it was a priority for the department. We get rocks. We get eggs. Spray paint. Death threats. Lotta death threats.

ANDY. Wow.

DEE. Phone rings five or six times a day. We don't answer anymore.

ANDY. Right.

   DEE *picks up the aluminium bat by the front door.*

DEE. That's why we keep this implement by the front door.

ANDY (*attempting conversation*). And and and... so how did you guys, um – ?

DEE. How did we – ?

ANDY. – ya know, wind up in – I mean – ?

DEE. It's a group home. You know what that is, right?

ANDY. No, I understand, but –

DEE. When you're on the registry there's a lotta rules about where you can and can't live and if you don't have anywhere else sometimes you get placed in a group home. That's how it works.

ANDY. Right. I just mean, ya know – Could be worse.

DEE. Don't you ever pity me, you smug bastard.

   ANDY *stares, unsure of* DEE*'s meaning.*

   Glenn Close. *Fatal Attraction.*

ANDY (*relieved*). Oh oh oh.

DEE. I was a performer.

ANDY. Oh wow.

DEE. Musical theater, primarily. National tours –

ANDY. Right.

DEE. – and a brief stint as assistant choreographer on two
    music videos featuring Vanessa Williams.

ANDY. Wow.

DEE. But we get a lotta broken windows. Even had a burning
    cross, on a special occasion.

ANDY. Well. Lotta hateful people in the world.

DEE. Oh honey I hate the *majority* of people.

ANDY. I don't believe that.

DEE. Remember Ronald Reagan?

ANDY. Um. *President* Reagan?

DEE. *Oh* I hated that man.

ANDY. Well –

DEE. Only President in American history with a face like
    a scrotum.

ANDY. Well, you know. I try not to hate people – whenever
    possible.

DEE. Your parents? Never hate your parents?

ANDY. No.

DEE. Huh.

ANDY. Never.

DEE. See, I think it's healthy for children to hate their parents.
    I think it's a necessary part of the maturation process.

ANDY. Well, I didn't hate mine. And my child – I mean, he gets
    angry, ya know, if we have to *discipline* him –

DEE. He never said *Daddy I hate you*?

ANDY (*shrugs*). Maybe in *anger*, but –

DEE. It's always in *anger*.

ANDY. Not always.

DEE. If you're telling somebody you *hate* them, then, *ipso facto* – ?

ANDY. No. Children experiment with words. But ya know, they exist in a state of innocence so they don't have the cognitive awareness to understand the impact of those words.

DEE. Mm-hmm.

ANDY. It's true.

DEE. When I was five years old my mother took me to the Kroger and I said Momma will you buy me this little plastic dinosaur filled with candy corn and she said no I will not, cuz that candy corn will rot the teeth outta your head so when she wasn't looking I took that little dinosaur and put it in my back pocket – and I *knew* it was wrong, ya understand. I knew perfectly well, but I just walked right outta that store, holding her hand, smiling and everything, and the next day she found that little dinosaur under my bed and said Dee, did you take that dinosaur after I told you not to and I said *no* Momma, I would *never* – all shocked and innocent, ya know. So she beat my ass cuz not only did I *steal* the dinosaur but then I *lied* about it.

ANDY. Right, well –

DEE. I was *never* in a state of innocence.

ANDY. – still, I don't think corporal punishment… is ever –

DEE. You don't hit your child.

ANDY. We generally do like a time out. He goes to his room.

DEE. Incarceration.

ANDY (*laughs*). Um.

DEE. How ya feel about the death penalty?

ANDY. Well –

DEE. Not for your *child*.

ANDY. It's a complicated –

DEE. I *support* the death penalty.

ANDY. – conceivably, in the most extreme –

DEE. Terrorists?

ANDY. – circumstances?

DEE. Serial killers?

ANDY. But I think *corporal* punishment actually, ya know, encourages *vengeance* rather than justice and I think the desire for revenge is something that we oughta, you know, try to discourage. Ideally.

DEE. So, *capital* punishment, yes, *corporal* punishment, no.

ANDY. It's not a contradiction.

DEE. It's not?

ANDY. No – I mean, yeah, I think some things can be worse than – ya know.

DEE. Worse than *death*?

ANDY. Lotta things worse than death.

DEE. Such as?

ANDY. …physical abuse?

DEE. Is *worse*.

ANDY. Torture.

DEE. Than *death*.

ANDY. Rape.

DEE. Is worse than *death*.

ANDY. Can be.

DEE (*clarifying*). You're saying being *raped* is *worse* than –

ANDY. I *am* saying that.

DEE. – now, I'm not saying rape is *good* –

ANDY. Depending on the victim, yes. Can be worse –

DEE. On the *victim*.

ANDY. – and I think we have a responsibility to protect the weakest and most vulnerable among us – Children, obviously. Women. (*With a gesture to* DEE.) People of color –

ANDY*'s cellphone begins to ring.*

(*Checking the screen as he talks.*) – I think the rest of us have, yeah, an obligation to defend those who can't always – defend – sorry –

ANDY *answers, lowering his voice.*

(*Sotto, into phone.*) – Hey. No, I was just – Yeah, I knocked on the door and they just – no, wasn't even there. (*Beat.*) Um. Sitting at the bar. Watching the game. Yeah, and, uh – talking to a guy. Yeah. Sox by two.

DEE *rises, exits into kitchen.*

(*Into phone.*) Well, did he go to sleep? Right? Did he take his – ? No no no. Don't wait for me. You're exhausted. I mean, Maria's in the room with him, right? So if he wakes up and – yeah, I tucked him in. Yeah we read for ten or fifteen – *Big Hungry Bear.*

DEE *returns from the kitchen with an aerosol can of Febreze. He walks the length of the room, filling the air with the spray.*

Yeah – Middle of the sixth, so, I don't know – hour and a half? Cool. I'll try not to wake you up. Okay.

ANDY *hangs up.* DEE *returns to his spot.*

DEE. Your wife doesn't know where you are?

ANDY. No, I told her where I – I told her I was –

DEE. Which hotel you staying at?

ANDY *is about to respond, doesn't.*

Gotta be either Best Western or the Red Roof but I don't see y'all staying at a Red Roof.

ANDY. Um –

DEE. Anyway.

ANDY. Anyway.

DEE. You were saying.

ANDY (*beat*). What was I saying?

DEE. Rape is worse than death.

ANDY. Right. And look. I know that some of you – Those of you
– I understand the system isn't always fair, and maybe
sometimes we err on the side of safety, and if in doing that we
occasionally go too far and and and deprive someone like
yourself of basic rights in a way that is disproportionate to –
well shame on us and maybe we should look at that but I think
it's to some extent excusable because it reflects, you know, the
priority we rightly place on children. As I think we should.

DEE. Mm-hm.

ANDY. And in my group – one of the things we we we've been
talking about in our survivors' group, this whole past year, is
how we struggle with a, um, misplaced sense of guilt for the
punishment that's brought on our behalf against our abusers.
But what's the alternative, you know?

DEE. *Survivors'* group.

ANDY. Survivors' network.

DEE. Well, I don't mean to quibble with your usage, but
wouldn't a *survivor* be like if ya survived a *plane crash* – ?

ANDY. No.

DEE. – as in, *not deceased*?

ANDY. Or survived a traumatic experience.

DEE (*beat*). Well, of course you *survived* it –

ANDY. That's not true –

DEE. – not a lotta cases of death by blowjob.

ANDY (*not having fully heard* DEE). – trauma – what?

DEE. Nothing.

ANDY. There's research – the brain gets rewired and the connections, the emotional circuitry gets severed, but but but we now *know* that you can actively reset those neurochemical… pathways by – by taking *ownership* of the negative memories, right? And using them to reframe the narrative and and and your long-term survival is to some extent dependent upon… I mean, I had a sense of self and and and and self-worth, and that was taken away from me, right? It was *stolen*. And there've been times, in the past, when… yeah. I've felt that I would have preferred to have been killed.

DEE. Really.

ANDY. Many times.

DEE. To be *murdered*.

ANDY. Might've been preferable, yeah.

DEE. Well ya know, I'm not a specialist or anything, but it sounds to me like maybe you're *depressed* –

ANDY. Not true.

DEE. – don'tcha think?

ANDY. No. It's *exponentially* – it's it's it's – cuz *death*? For some of us? Is actually seen as a release, yeah, from… from the pain we feel.

DEE. But, logically speaking, you wouldn't feel *nothing* if you're *dead* –

ANDY. Exactly.

DEE. – whereas, if you're *alive*, see, there's always a chance the situation might *improve*.

ANDY (*polite, rational*). Except you've never *been* in my situation. Have you?

DEE. I've been *depressed*.

ANDY. But you don't know what I've been through, okay?
    So you can't possibly know what I feel.

DEE. When I was four years old the Allen County Sheriff's
    Department removed me from my grandparents' house cuz
    the Sunday School teacher found bruises on my neck.

ANDY. Um, I didn't – wow. I'm very sorry.

DEE. But I don't wish I was *dead*.

ANDY. But you carry the pain.

DEE. Oh honey, I barely remember.

ANDY (*condescending laugh*). Umm – I'm pretty sure you do.

DEE (*sincerely*). I really don't.

ANDY. Somewhere.

DEE. I'm doing just fine.

ANDY. Well – (*Polite laugh.*) I mean… obviously *not*. I mean,
    look around, right? Look where you wound up. And, I don't
    know – maybe if you'd had the chance to look a little
    deeper? Or or or or talk to someone – ?

DEE. A doctor, ya mean?

ANDY. – someone who could maybe see past some of your
    defenses – ?

DEE. Doctors *I* go to tell me *I'm* the problem, see, whereas
    doctors *you* go to tell ya somebody *else* is the problem.

ANDY. Somebody else *was* the problem.

DEE. Maybe the *doctor's* the problem.

ANDY. And I don't know if you know this? But seventy-six
    percent of predators were victimized themselves in
    childhood. That's just a fact. Those are the numbers. And
    those victims go on, in turn, to victimize others.

DEE. Is that right?

ANDY. Seventy-six percent.

DEE. Your child better lock his door tonight.

>ANDY *stares coldly*. DEE *smiles*.

>Honey, I'm *teasing* you.

ANDY (*unamused*). Uh-huh. Uh-huh. Well, I actually came to see Fred, so –

DEE. And ya know, if you're so unhappy being *alive* you could rectify that situation any time.

ANDY. I *have* considered suicide, okay? I actually have.

DEE (*dismissive*). Oh, everybody *considers* it.

ANDY. No. I made a *plan*.

DEE (*enumerating*). I had to have my stomach pumped twice –

ANDY. I was in such extreme –

DEE. – had to get eleven stitches in my *wrists* –

ANDY (*trying to end it*). Things were *done* to me. Okay? When I was a *child*. You understand what I'm saying? Without my consent.

*punishment
v. other
kinds of
harm*

DEE. Course you didn't *consent*. When does a *child* ever consent? Children don't consent to go to school, don't consent to take a bath, go to church, say the pledge of allegiance –

ANDY. You're not hearing me.

DEE. I hear you.

ANDY. I don't think you do.

DEE. I just reject the validity of your premise.

ANDY. I was twelve years old, okay?

DEE. I know what happened to you.

ANDY. Well, apparently you don't.

>DEE *raises his eyebrows, sips his tea*.

Or maybe you know what Fred says? But you know what? Fred's a *liar*. As we know. That's what you guys do. You lie, you manipulate the truth to your advantage, you groom your victims, so why should anybody ever believe a single word you say, since by definition, it will always be a *lie*?

DEE. I had a sexual relationship with a fourteen-year-old boy when I was thirty-seven.

ANDY (*even*). Uh-huh.

DEE. *I'm* not lyin' to you.

ANDY. Uh-huh. (*Judiciously.*) Well. Ya know. I think that's… pretty… reprehensible. But look. I don't know. People make mistakes –

DEE. For two and a half years. We had sex on multiple occasions over the course of two and a half years.

ANDY. Okay, well –

DEE. It was the 1998 national tour of *Peter Pan* starring Miss Cathy Rigby –

ANDY. I don't want to know.

DEE. – for which I was both dance captain and one of the pirates on *The Jolly Roger*. And the young man with whom I had this relationship –

ANDY. It's *not* a relationship.

DEE. – was portraying one of the Lost Boys by the name of 'Tootles' –

ANDY. Okay, first of all –

DEE. – and you know, he sent me a handwritten letter every single week for six years after I was sent away, telling me how much he missed me –

ANDY. First of all, it's not a young man, it's a *child*, okay? And secondly, it's not a relationship, it's it's it's – I mean, *Jesus Christ* – and third? That you can be unaware of that – ? It's *exploitation*, okay? However you wanna – It's *abuse*. And if

you can't *see* that? Especially *now*? With everything we – ?
I mean – *Wow*. That's… astonishing. And yes, I think it's
entirely reasonable that we, as a society should punish that.

DEE. I went to prison for fifteen years.

ANDY. Well. I think that's more or less appropriate.

DEE (*interesting fact*). Did you know there's six states tried to
enact the *death penalty* for rapin' a child?

ANDY. I really don't care.

DEE. Now, that ain't possible cuzza the Supreme Court – but
they *tried*.

ANDY. Right. Well –   *special status of sex offenses*

DEE. And in those states, see, you could break both your child's
legs with a sledgehammer, if you felt like it. Dunk that baby
in boiling oil – long as that child don't end up *dead* you can't
get the death penalty. Now, on the other hand, if you ever
happen to suck that child's *dick* –

ANDY. Okay, you know what?

DEE. – you'd be better off *amputating* that dick than *sucking* it.
You say I'm sorry your honor I lost control of myself, I cut
off my child's dick and put it in the food processor – Judge'd
be like alright that's twenty months for criminal assault and
it's a shame your child's gotta live without a *dick* the rest of
his life, but thank *god* you didn't *suck* that dick –

ANDY. It's not funny.

Dee is more competent/prepared as a jailhouse lawyer. he's had this argument before – he's a repeat player

DEE (*continuous*). – cuz if you *did*? Judge'll give ya *twenty
years*, for that –

Headlights outside. Car doors slam.

ANDY. I was *assaulted*, okay? It was an *act of violence*.

DEE. Ya mean an old man sucked your dick.

ANDY. I was *raped* by a *serial predator*. It was a *criminal act*.

DEE. Oh honey. If suckin' dicks was a crime I'd be Al Capone.

We hear GIO *and* EFFIE *approaching the open front door, mid-squabble –*

GIO *(quietly, from off).* – yeah, but we're not talking about *money –*

EFFIE *(quietly overlapping, from off).* Of course you're talking about money. It's all you *ever* talk about.

GIO *(continuous).* – we're talking about doing something constructive with your life, and if money's all you think a career means then you are sadly mistaken – and who left the front door standin' open to the fuckin' world? *(Calling out as they enter.) Felix!*

EFFIE *and* GIO *enter with pizza in a box.*

EFFIE. Which is the bathroom?

GIO. On the left – *(Spotting* ANDY.*)* whoops –

EFFIE. Oh my god, oh my god, oh my god –

EFFIE *crosses to bathroom –* DEE *stands, quietly alarmed.* GIO *sucks up to* ANDY.

GIO. – didn't see ya. How're ya doing this evening? *(Extending hand.)* Giovanni Joseph. Made our introductions earlier this morning.

ANDY. Hi.

GIO. To what do we owe the pleasure?

ANDY *(not wanting the interaction).* Um –

GIO *(remembering).* Oh! – left your phone behind.

ANDY *(showing phone).* I did.

GIO. iPhone X.

ANDY. Exactly.

GIO. Didn't catch your name – ?

ANDY. Andy.

GIO. – you and your lovely wife. And her name was – ?

ANDY. I'm actually just waiting for Fred –

GIO (*to* DEE, *on* ANDY*'s behalf*). What happened to Fred?

DEE. He's late.

GIO *shuts the front door, turns off fan.*

GIO (*to* ANDY). Can we getcha something to drink? (*To* DEE.) Why'ntcha get him something to drink?

DEE (*quietly grave*). May I speak to you please?

GIO (*ignoring* DEE). And I hope this won't bother ya but I was obliged to work through the dinner hour and I don't like to enjoy myself in front of company – (*Re: pizza.*) so I wonder if I might interest you in a piece of this – ?

ANDY. No thanks.

GIO. – half-sausage half-mushroom? Now, the young woman's in charge of the mushroom half but if you're a carnivore help yourself. *Felix, let's go.*

GIO *crosses into kitchen,* DEE *follows.* ANDY *can overhear the quiet conversation coming from inside the kitchen.*

DEE (*sotto as they exit*). I'd like to speak to you.

GIO (*sotto, from off*). Where's Felix at?

DEE (*sotto, from off*). What is that girl doing here?

GIO (*sotto, from off*).) I asked you first.

DEE (*sotto, from off*). I don't *know* where he is.

GIO (*sotto, from off*). Didn't go to *work*, did he*?*

DEE (*sotto, from off*). I told you I don't know.

GIO (*sotto, from off*). Felix don't work *Saturday.*

DEE (*sotto, from off*). Will you answer the question, please?

GIO *returns with a roll of paper towels, cans of soda,* DEE *following behind.*

GIO (*ignoring* DEE, *to* ANDY). And if I remember correctly, you and Fred had some financial business to attend to, innat right? –

GIO *grabs a slice of pizza and a napkin and settles in near* ANDY. DEE *hovers, waiting to speak to* GIO *alone.*

(*Continuous, to* ANDY .) – least, Fred said something about you havin' a connection to the financial industry – cuz lemme say upfront I gotta lotta respect for that. Financial services gotta lotta negative press back in 2008 with the mortgage crisis and the ninety-nine percent, and alla that notwithstanding I happen to be of the opinion that wealth creation is a necessary evil –

GIO *takes a bite, talks as he chews –*

– cuz we got ourselves a problem in this country – I'll come right out and say it – too many folks going around, playing the victim, refuse to empower themselves with the proverbial bootstraps – Cuz we all been through a rough patch, every now and then, right? Person such as myself – I had my dark period. Circumstances kept me outta the job market a number of years, but I put that time to positive use. Gotta certificate of business administration from Kaplan University online, and I emerged a stronger person both mentally *and* spiritually – cuz some people think faith and business are incompatible, but that's a common misconception. Cuz ya know Christ himself was a small businessman. That's true. Had himself a thriving carpentry business before being called to higher service –

Toilet flush.

(*Continuous.*) – and I'm currently planning to relocate to the Chicago area myself, develop a distribution platform for product delivery and I'm in the process of raising the necessary capital to take it to the next level.

ANDY. Um, what's the… product?

GIO. Uhh, that is yet to be determined, but lemme askya a question –

EFFIE *returns from the bathroom.*

– that's your car out there in the driveway, innit? Audi Q7?

ANDY. Yeah.

GIO. And I support that choice. Germany's a world leader in manufacturing technology, but lemme askya this –

EFFIE. Omigod I almost pee'd my pants.

EFFIE *takes a slice of pizza, sits near* GIO *and* ANDY.

GIO. – what'd be the average starting price, car like that? The MSRP?

ANDY. I don't know.

GIO. I'm gonna guess, forty-five, fifty K – that sound about right?

ANDY. I don't know.

GIO. Cuz that would exceed my present budget, but I'm setting up a savings and pension plan through my place of business – you're familiar with the retail outlet known as Staples?

ANDY. Yeah.

GIO. Office Superstore?

ANDY. Staples, yeah.

GIO. Cuz I'm currently employed by the Staples corporation.

EFFIE (*to* ANDY). We work at Staples.

GIO. Ya know the Staples next to Chesterfield Mall? Next to the AutoZone?

ANDY. I'm from Chicago.

GIO. Anyway, it's entry-level, sales associate, but there's benefits and I see it as a transitional stepping-stone out of the service sector into some kinda managerial capacity?

EFFIE (*eating pizza*). Omigod, Gio, you're like the worst employee *ever*.

GIO. Not true.

EFFIE (*to* ANDY). He undercounts the inventory on the shipping manifest? And he takes the overstock home with him – ?

GIO. Not true.

EFFIE. – and he proselytizes about his religion to rest of the sales staff? (*To* GIO.) And if I was Marcus I would like totally fire you.

GIO. Well, these are fabrications, and if ya speak to Marcus directly I think you'll find he does not share your opinion –

EFFIE. Um? Marcus *hates* you.

GIO (*continuous*). – cuz I got people skills and work off my own initiative, unlike *your* lazy self –

EFFIE. Don't call me lazy.

GIO. – who is nothing but a detriment to the workplace –

EFFIE. Don't call me lazy.

GIO. – and I will *continue* to call you lazy cuz you're one of the most lethargic individuals I ever seen –

EFFIE. A workplace is a safe space.

GIO. – standing around with your head stuck in your phone textin' your friends –

EFFIE. A workplace is a safe space.

GIO (*continuous*). – when you're sposeta be out on the floor makin' *sales* – and we're not *at* the workplace so why'ntchoo shut the fuck up? (*To* ANDY.) 'Scuse my language.

DEE (*to* GIO). If I may interrupt?

GIO (*ignoring* DEE, *to* ANDY). Tellya something else. Workplace like that. Kinda things that happen on a daily basis? Comedic situations? Somebody oughta make a situation comedy set in a Staples franchise –

EFFIE. Omigod this woman today – ?

GIO. – I oughta copyright that idea, pitch it to Showtime or something.

EFFIE. – she's like – (*Nasally imitation.*) *I lost my receipt but Customer Service told me I have store credit and you have to honor that.*

GIO. No *receipt.*

EFFIE. She's like *I'm taking my business to Office Depot cuz they don't disrespect their customers and you just lost your commission.*

GIO. And I'm like *bitch* – 'scuse my language – I'm like *woman, I will personally give you a piggyback ride to Office Depot if it'll get your ass outta my store.*

DEE. Excuse me?

EFFIE. Why is there a *stench* in here?

GIO (*smelling it*). *Aw god.*

EFFIE. It's like *rancid.*

GIO. Fuck *is* that?

DEE. May I speak to you privately, please?

GIO *stands to reopen the front door and turn the fan back on. As he does:*

GIO (*ignoring* DEE, *to* ANDY). Sir, you wouldn't happen to be a competitive bridge player, by any chance?

ANDY. I'm actually just –

GIO. Cuz we're gonna be playin' with another one of our residents, dollar a hand, and I'll tellya what – (*Re:* EFFIE.) this girl may look all young and innocent but she is a deadly adversary.

EFFIE. It's true.

GIO. She will take you for everything you got.

GIO *disappears into kitchen,* DEE *following.*

EFFIE (*to* ANDY). So I'm kind of like this *math* genius?

ANDY (*checking the time*). Uh-huh.

EFFIE. Cuz we had an assessment when I was in school and I tested like in the highest percentile on the math section, but I was also diagnosed with ADHD and interstitial cystitis which is where you have to pee really frequently, and I also have a lot of anxiety which is why I do below average on standardized tests? But it also means I'm really good at card games as long as I'm on my medication?

GIO (*audible from kitchen*). Nunna your fuckin' business how old she is.

EFFIE. Like you can ask me like a really complex problem using derivative functions and I can solve it in my head like superfast without a pencil or anything – (*Without stopping.*) You know who you remind me of?

ANDY (*standing to leave*). Excuse me.

ANDY *heads for door as* GIO *and* DEE *return from kitchen, arguing quietly.*

DEE (*sotto, as they enter*). – and you are not having a little sleepover in this house, you understand me?

GIO *spots* ANDY *about to leave.*

GIO (*to* ANDY). Sir? Sir? Sir?

ANDY. Thanks. I'm gonna go.

GIO. Fred's gonna be along any second now.

ANDY. It's fine.

GIO. Shall we tell him you stopped by?

ANDY. No thanks.

GIO. Convey a message for ya?

ANDY. No.

GIO. Happy to do it.

ANDY. No thanks.

GIO. He's got your number?

ANDY. I don't know.

GIO. Got your email? Social media?

ANDY. I don't know.

And at that moment, FRED *rolls through the open door in his scooter.* GIO *spots him:*

GIO. Well, look at that. Whaddya know. Abracadabra. Right on cue.

FRED. What's the matter?

GIO. Evenin', Fred.

FRED. What's happening?

GIO. Fred – introduce you to my friend Effie –

EFFIE. I'm Effie.

GIO. – work colleague of mine – (*To* EFFIE.) You'll appreciate this – Fred's gotta musical background. Back in the day, used to be a pianist with a classical repertoire.

EFFIE (*to* FRED). I play the oboe.

DEE *closes door, turns off fan.*

GIO. So y'all got something in common. And I apologize, Fred, we been monopolizing this gentleman, invading his personal space, so the two of us, we're gonna go to *my* personal space, outta sight outta mind – cuz I know y'all got business to attend to and I respect that, cuz nothing's more important to a man than keeping his financial affairs in order –

EFFIE. Which way?

GIO. Straight ahead. And soon as Felix shows up y'all just tell him where we're at, alright?

EFFIE *takes pizza, opens door to* GIO*'s bedroom –*

EFFIE (*as she enters*). Omigod. It's disgusting in here.

GIO. Shut the fuck up.

They exit into the bedroom, slamming the door behind them.

FRED. What was all that about?

DEE. I have no idea.

FRED. Where's Felix?

DEE. I don't know.

FRED. Did he go to work?

DEE. I don't know.

FRED. And who is that girl?

DEE. I don't *know*, Fred.

FRED. I'm not sure that's a good idea.

DEE. It's a very *bad* idea.

DEE *goes to* GIO*'s closed door, surveilling.*

ANDY. Anyway –

FRED. – and *Andy* – oh golly – is Emily with you?

ANDY. No. She's –

FRED. We thought ya went back to Chicago.

ANDY. We decided to –

FRED. Oh oh – the *water park*!

ANDY. – right.

FRED. Didja make it to the water park?

ANDY. We did. Anyway – Um – It's just – Ya know – this morning we were sitting here and, um, I never felt like I really got the chance to to to, um –

FRED. Oh I *know*.

ANDY. – really articulate the the the... full extent of –

FRED. All the *interruptions*.

ANDY (*continuous*). – what I've been – cuz I guess I was just feeling – I don't know – reluctant or whatever –

DEE *crosses back toward kitchen*.

DEE. Want your Swiss Miss, Fred?

FRED. Oh golly yes please if you wouldn't mind – Andy, I don't suppose you want some hot cocoa?

ANDY. No.

DEE *enters kitchen*.

FRED. I know it's the middle of the summer and everything but for some reason I can just never fall asleep at night until – Oh – didja find your *phone*?

ANDY *holds up the phone*.

We got so worried, you know – We saw it sitting there and we didn't have any way to get it back to ya and I said to everyone, I said ya know what, I betcha Andy'll realize he left it behind and come back for it. And here ya are.

ANDY. Anyway –

FRED. Sure hope you haven't been waiting too long.

ANDY. No.

FRED. Cuz normally we're done by eight-thirty – (*Remembering*.) Oh, oh Andy!

ANDY. What?

FRED. Ya know what I remembered this morning?

ANDY. When?

FRED. See if you remember this – wait a second. It just popped into my head right after you left.

FRED *swivels the joystick, wheels himself toward the CD player*.

Cuz the two of you drove away and I was sitting here and this little tune just popped into my head and I was thinking, well, now why did that pop into my head all of a sudden like that – ?

FRED *hits play on the CD player. The 'Raindrop' Prelude begins to play.*

– remember that?

ANDY. Sure, yeah.

FRED. Ya know what that is?

ANDY. Chopin.

FRED. Remember how you learned that practically all by yourself – ?

ANDY. I do.

FRED. – without hardly any help from me? Cuz that's not an easy piece for someone that age but you just picked it up real quick and that was very advanced and that's why I thought you woulda kept up with your playing because you just had a natural ability and that's very special –

ANDY. Well –

FRED. Shame to let that go to waste.

ANDY. – anyway.

FRED. He had kind of a tragic life, you know. Chopin, I mean.

ANDY. Right.

FRED. He fell in love with the wrong woman and the family rejected him and they called off the engagement and oh he was heartbroken for the rest of –

ANDY. I remember, yeah.

FRED. You know that story?

ANDY. Yeah, you told it to me when I was like, eleven.

FRED. Oh.

FRED *switches off the CD. Music stops.*

I got this little keyboard – Not the same as the real thing but it's a pretty neat little deal. And I can't play like I used to with the arthritis and everything but I follow along with the sheet music and kinda run my fingers over the keys and whenever I'm feeling sorry for myself boy I tellya that just cheers me up a whole bunch –

ANDY. What uh, happened to your piano?

FRED. Oh golly. I hope it went to some nice family or something. Maybe just got turned into firewood, I really couldn't tell ya. (*Beat.*) Remember how Tommy – cuz he was younger than you, ya know, and I remember one time he said I sure hope those white keys aren't made outta real ivory from elephants. He got real upset about that and I said I didn't think so and he was relieved cuzza elephants being endangered and all.

DEE *has returned from kitchen with mug of instant cocoa, pills and a plate of cookies.*

DEE. Putting this here for ya, Fred.

FRED. Thank you for that.

DEE. Don't forget your pills. And here's your Nutter Butters.

DEE *exits to kitchen again.*

FRED. Ohhh. Remember these, Andy? How we used to have these?

ANDY. Yeah.

FRED. These Nutter Butters cookies?

ANDY. I remember.

FRED. Do ya still have those?

ANDY. No.

FRED. Oh I sure do. And Tommy – He was so fulla beans. He'd always want to have his Nutter Butter before we'd even started and I'd have to say hold your horses, we gotta save those till after we're done! (*Smiles.*) That used to make me laugh because he sure loved those Nutter Butters.

ANDY. Are you talking about Tom Rizley?

FRED. You're probably not in touch with him, I don't imagine.

ANDY. Why would I be in touch with him?

FRED (*beat*). I don't know. You got in touch with *me*.

ANDY. I have no contact with him.

FRED. Okay.

ANDY. Last I heard I think he was living in Paris.

FRED. That's what I heard.

ANDY. With his partner.

FRED. I heard that too.

ANDY. In fact I think they got married.

FRED. And so did you.

ANDY. Right. (*Beat.*) To a *man*. I meant Tom got married to –

FRED. I knew what you meant.

ANDY. – his partner – husband, right.

FRED. Well, good for him. I sure do hope he's doing okay.

ANDY. Apparently he's fine.

FRED. I wonder if *he* still plays piano?

ANDY. I would have no way of knowing.

FRED *moves the joystick of his chair – it doesn't respond.*

FRED. Oh boy. This gosh-darn chair –

ANDY (*half-attempting to help*). Do you need – um – ?

FRED. – never seems to wanta go where ya – (*Solving it.*) Whoops, there we go.

ANDY. How long have you been, um, using a – ?

FRED. Oh golly. When did I – ? Nineteen ninety… *seven*?

ANDY. And did the doctors – was it like, some kind of –
    degenerative – ?

FRED. Ohhh. (*Beat.*) Guess ya never heard that story.

ANDY. Guess not.

FRED. Doesn't really matter now.

ANDY. Well –

FRED. There was a man. And well, he didn't care for me very
    much.

ANDY. Uh-huh.

FRED. I guess he'd read about… things I did… to you and
    Tommy – and ya know, it was so good they never printed
    either of your names. They were real careful about that, cuz
    you were both so young and they wanted to protect you and
    that was real smart of them. It really was. (*Beat.*) Anyway
    this man, he'd read about all that and I guess that's why he
    was so angry. Or maybe it was just my personality, but…
    (*Beat, matter-of-fact.*) He broke my back. My spinal column.

ANDY (*even*). Huh.

FRED. Yeah. And he was wearing boots, which is funny, ya
    know, because you're not supposed to have boots in there,
    you're supposed to wear sneakers or slip-ons or flip-flops but
    somehow he managed to get hold of some of those kinda
    steel-toed work boots, and he just kept on kicking and
    stomping till I was in pretty bad shape. And then he kicked
    me in the mouth, so I lost a coupla teeth. But you can always
    get new teeth.

ANDY. Um. I didn't know any of that.

FRED. Oh yeah. So I don't walk anymore, and I get a kinda
    pain in my legs sometimes, and I can't really control when
    I go to the bathroom, so I need a little help now and then but

I tellya what, I get around pretty good in this old chair, and
Dee helps me out around here and boy oh boy I just
appreciate that a whole heckuva lot.

ANDY. And. Um. Is your… wife – Is Bonnie – ?

FRED. Oh no no no. She died quite a while ago.

ANDY. I didn't know that either.

FRED. Oh sure. Kidney failure. But we'd stopped talking a
long time before that. So I guess it's a lucky thing we never
had kids of our own, but you know, the truth of it is, Andy,
I'm doing just fine. I really am. And I can't tell ya how much
it means to me that you came all this way –

ANDY. Yeah, but – (*Cold laugh.*) I mean – It's not like I'm
doing this for *you.*

FRED. Well, sure, I –

ANDY. That's not the point of it.

FRED. Okay.

Pause.

So, what *is* the – [point of it]?

ANDY. I mean, I don't know if you expect me to, feel, like,
what? I dunno, some kind of *sympathy,* or – ?

FRED. No no no.

ANDY. – or, or *compassion*, or something?

FRED. Oh no.

ANDY. Cuz that's not gonna happen.

FRED. Okay.

ANDY. You're not the victim, okay?

FRED. I know that.

ANDY. And in our group – I mean, this whole past year has
really been such a, a, a… watershed – for all of us, you

know, not just for women – and one of the things they try to
teach you is, whenever you do a confrontation –

FRED. Is this a confrontation?

ANDY (*beat*). What did you *think* it was?

FRED. I didn't know *what* to think.

due process
R to confront
witnesses

Pause.

I mean, gosh I was just so surprised, ya know, to find that
letter in the mailbox outta the blue like that with your name
there on the envelope – I don't even know how ya got the
address –

ANDY (*incredulous*). Well, I mean – it's *published*.

FRED. Oh sure.

ANDY. It's *online*. It's like two clicks. And all of a sudden it's
like oh look – there he is again. Out in the world, ya know?
And does anyone bother to inform *me* of that?

FRED. Well –

ANDY. I mean, you'd think they'd have to *notify* you or – cuz if
I hadn't bothered to look it up – I mean, I thought you were
still in the –?

FRED. Correctional center.

treatment +
pathology

ANDY. – the place in Evansville?

FRED. Well, that's civil commitment, ya know. That's
voluntary, after you get released. But eventually ya have to
transition out of there, too, so –

ANDY. I mean, you really don't have any *idea*, do you? What
this *feels* like – That for the rest of my life – to have this
awareness that this person is is is is always going to be *out
there* somewhere – ?

FRED. Andy –

ANDY. – I mean, do you have any appreciation of how that
feels?

FRED. Andy. Listen to me. I wantcha to listen, now. (*Slowly.*) What I did... was very *wrong* –

ANDY. Uh-huh. Uh-huh.

FRED. – It was a terrible, *terrible* thing. And I understand that now. I really do –

ANDY. Right. Right.

FRED. – no – Andy, *listen* to me. People like me, we have a sickness. And we do bad things to people because we have a problem with our thinking and we hurt people real bad just like I hurt you and Tommy. And I don't know why the Lord would make me this way –

ANDY. Yeah, let's not drag 'the Lord' into it, okay?

FRED. Okay.

ANDY. You were an *adult*. You made *choices*. And we're not actually *talking* about *you*, okay?

FRED. Okay

ANDY. We're talking about *me* –

FRED. Okay.

ANDY. – and, what *I* went through, and truth of it is? I think it's an act. This whole gee-whiz-golly-gee bullshit – I don't think you've changed at all. I see no evidence of that whatsoever –

FRED (*beat*). Well –

ANDY. – meanwhile *some* of us, ya know, those of us who can barely get out of bed in the morning with with with the shame and the guilt and the anger –

FRED. Oh Andy.

ANDY. – I have *serious issues*, okay? Are you aware of that? I have *trust* issues. Issues with *intimacy*? I get these these, these *episodes* – I had to take kickboxing and kendo, you know, just to have some kind of outlet for the the the the ... *rage* and the feelings of hopelessness –

FRED (*sympathetically*). Ohhh.

ANDY. – I just get overwhelmed, you know? With like, the tiniest little trigger. Like at the gym, or work – just sitting there at my desk –

FRED. At your bank –

ANDY (*whispered, teeth gritted*). – *it is NOT a bank, okay?* –

FRED. Okay.

ANDY (*whispered fury*). *And can you PLEASE not interrupt me?*

FRED. Okay.

ANDY (*likewise*). *Is that too much to ask? To fucking listen for once in your life?*

FRED. I'm listening.

ANDY (*same*). *Fuck.*

DEE, *unseen, calls from the kitchen.*

DEE (*from off*). Everybody alright?

FRED. Everything's fine.

DEE. Ya sure?

FRED. Oh sure.

DEE *slides into the kitchen door.*

DEE. Either of y'all need anything?   *not checking on felix*

FRED. No no no.

DEE. Marshmallow for your Swiss Miss?

FRED. No thanks.

DEE. You sure?

FRED. Thank you, though.

DEE. Alright.

DEE *slides back into the kitchen*.

ANDY (*calmer now*). Now I lost my [train of thought] –

FRED. At the bank.

ANDY. It's *not* a bank, okay? It's not a bank.

FRED. Okay

ANDY. It's not.

FRED. Not a bank.

ANDY (*beat*). Financial management.

FRED. Okay.

ANDY. It's – It's – It's – you know, it's a way of helping people – people who, yeah, maybe have a little money and don't know the best way to –

FRED. I bet that's a big help.

ANDY. – cuz who was ever there for *me*, you know? When *I* needed help?

FRED. Without your dad.

ANDY. After he died, yeah, and my mom being so emotionally –

FRED. You were sensitive.

ANDY. – unavailable – I mean, had *anyone* been there – which is why I'm trying to *help* people now, ya know, to give back in some way, even if it's… financially – at least I'm doing *something*.

FRED. Well, Andy, I'm just so *proud* of everything you've ac–

ANDY (*holding back tears*). Well, *I don't feel proud*, okay?

FRED (*soothing*). I know.

ANDY. I haven't felt proud for thirty years.

FRED. I know.

ANDY. I can't even – Emily has to pick out my *clothes*. I'll be standing there – she's like what the fuck is wrong with you? It's *eight-fifteen*. Like I'm not even in my own body. Like I'm outside myself, like going through the motions – and how do you explain that to a *child*, ya know? How do you say I don't even know who I'm supposed to be half the time? How do you say that to a five-year-old child, huh? How do I do that?

FRED (*slow, thoughtfully*). Well, ya know… it's funny – I think maybe a *lotta* people feel some of those things, don'tcha think –

ANDY. No they don't. No they don't –

FRED. – from time to time?

[handwritten: judicial/court/formal process traumatic in itself..]

ANDY. – and you know *why* they don't? Because they didn't have to sit in front of a *judge* – Do you have any concept – At *twelve*? Before I'd even held hands with a girl? To *describe* how some some some older *man* had – have you ever *once* thought about how that *felt* –

FRED. I think about it all the time.

ANDY (*continuous*). – to *strangers* in a *courtroom*? Sitting next to me on the piano bench with your hand resting on my – cuz, what I *should* have done, ya know, I should've just jumped up and beat your fucking *face* in.

DEE *crosses past the kitchen, door, briefly visible. ANDY lowers his voice.*

I couldn't even go *home*. I was so – I got on my bike and rode away like *praying* none of my friends would see me and I hid in that drainage ditch behind the Methodist church, like… *shaking*. For *hours*. My whole body. Tears like *burning* my face I was so fucking ashamed and I waited until it was dark and I rode home and went behind our garage and took my pants off and threw my underwear in the garbage cuz of how disgusting I – I couldn't even go inside for dinner. And when I finally do my mother's just sitting there reading a magazine like like… like she didn't even fucking *notice* – ?

He breaks down crying like a child. FRED *lets it go on for a while, then reaches out and touches* ANDY.

(*In tears.*) ...*like she didn't even care.*

FRED (*kindly*). Oh Andy.

ANDY. *I thought you cared about me, you know?*

FRED. I did care –

ANDY. *No you didn't.*

FRED. – sure I did.

ANDY. *You told me you were my friend.*

FRED. I still am.

ANDY. *You said I was special. That's what you said.*

FRED. And I meant it.

ANDY. *No you didn't.*

FRED. You *are* special.

ANDY. *But you said the same thing to Tommy.*

FRED. Well –

ANDY. *Why did you lie to me?*

FRED It wasn't a lie.

ANDY. *You told him the exact same thing.*

FRED. You were both special.

ANDY. *You fucking liar.*

FRED. Shhhhhh, now...

DEE *has entered quietly at a distance. When he speaks,* ANDY *sobers up, wipes his eyes, moves away from* FRED.

DEE (*gently*). How we doin' here?

ANDY (*regaining control*). Sorry.

FRED. Oh, we're fine. We're doing just fine.

DEE. Well, I just wanted to check and see.

FRED. Thank you, though.

DEE (*to* FRED). Ya feeling tired?

FRED. Nooo.

DEE. Ya *look* a little tired.

FRED. I'm *fine*.

DEE. Alright.

FRED (*soothing*). Everybody's *fine*.

DEE. But... (*Carefully.*) maybe that's about enough for one night, don'tcha think?

FRED. Well, I want make sure Andy gets to say everything he wants to.

DEE. I understand.

FRED. As long as he gets to do that.

DEE (*gently, to* ANDY). So, you feel like you said everything you wanna say?

ANDY (*cold, rational*). Well, um, no. As a matter of fact, I don't.

DEE. Alright. (*Beat.*) So why'ntcha go ahead and do that, then?

ANDY (*controlled*). Well. Um. Maybe I *could* do that, ya know, if I wasn't, uh, being constantly interrupted?

DEE (*beat*). Honey, I know you're upset, and I know there's a lotta feelings, but it is getting kinda late now, and Fred's gotta have his bath –

ANDY (*calm*). Well. I think those are decisions Fred can make for himself.

DEE (*beat*). Alright, let's ask Fred, then. You wanna keep talking, Fred, or you wanna take your bath?

FRED. Oh gosh. Ya know... I'm real sorry ya came all this way, Andy. I feel real bad about that, but... I'm not exactly sure what else it is you want me to –

ANDY *opens the manila envelope, pulls out the stapled pages.*

ANDY *(formal)*. Okay. So. This is called a reconciliation contract, okay? Way it works is, you present it to your – ya know – and they read it aloud and they can choose to reject it, but if you accept, then you make a formal admission of what you did, and pledge to take full responsibility for your actions, and never make contact with either your victims or their family –

ANDY. – either now or at any point in the –	DEE *(calmly)*. He didn't contact *you*. You contacted *him*.	FRED *(to DEE)*. Shh-sh-sh-sh. It's okay.

ANDY *(continuous, to DEE)*. – excuse me – excuse me?

DEE. Go ahead.

ANDY. And then sign at the bottom. So. *(Hands contract to FRED.)* If you wanna just uh, ya know, read that and… sign it when you're finished.

FRED *(peering at contract)*. Oh golly –

ANDY. I've got a pen.

FRED. – I'm gonna need my other glasses.

DEE. Fred? Tellya what. Why don't the two of us do this in the morning?

ANDY. Because I won't be here in the morning.

FRED *(to DEE)*. Because Andy won't be here in the –

DEE. Well, maybe we can send it to him in the mail, then.

ANDY. Well, that's not how it works.

DEE. Well, maybe it could this time.

ANDY. Well, maybe you're not the one who's in charge of the situation.

Pause. DEE and ANDY stare at each other.

DEE. Honey –

ANDY (*vaguely threatening*). I'm not twelve years old, okay? Understand what I'm saying? I'm actually a full-grown adult.

DEE. Is that supposed to make me afraid?

ANDY (*shrugs, calmly*). Take it however you want.

DEE (*beat*). Whatcha want, baby? Ya want money? –

ANDY. I don't need *money*.

DEE. – Cuz Fred ain't *got* any money.

ANDY. I want the *truth*. I want him to read that aloud, and admit what he did.

DEE. He *already* admitted it in a court of law –

DEE (*continuous*). – nearly thirty years ago, and he doesn't need to do it again tonight.	ANDY. I mean *everything*. Without leaving anything out this time –

ANDY (*continuous*). – and when he's finished he can sign it at the bottom.

FRED *puts on his reading glasses*.

FRED (*struggling to read*). I – golly – so I'm just supposed to read this out loud, then?

ANDY. Unless you're afraid of that.

FRED. No no. I'm – Uh. Let's see, now. So… starting here at the top – ?

ANDY. From the top.

FRED *reads haltingly, squinting through his glasses*.

FRED. – boy, that's a small font, isn't it? Uh – okay – Let's see – *I, Frederick Jerome Nyberg, do freely and of my… own –*

ANDY. – admission –

FRED. – *admission confess that on... two separate occasions in July of 1998 I did* – sado – oops – *sodomize and rape Andrew Wilmorth by oral contact with his penis, by insertion of* – this font is very – *insertion of my fingertip into his* – (*Handing contract to* DEE.) What does that – [say]?

DEE (*reading quietly over* FRED*'s shoulde*r). Anal cavity.

FRED. – oh oh, okay – in your bottom, okay –

ANDY. Right, and – ?

FRED (*innocently answering, not reading*). And... what?

ANDY. And what else?

FRED. And... that was very bad.

ANDY. No. What else *happened*?

FRED (*beat, confused*). Well... uhh, ya know, I got punished. And I *deserved* to [be punished] –

ANDY. No. I mean the thing that happened *next*.

FRED. Well, I'm not sure I know what you –

ANDY. Yes you do. Yes you do. You know exactly – I *know* you do. So maybe you could stop fucking around and read what it is you actually *did*.

DEE (*from contract*). He wants you to say you put your penis in his mouth.

ANDY. Hey. Hey.

DEE. Least, that's what it says *here* –

ANDY. Hey, man.   FRED (*troubled*). Ohhhhh.

DEE. – only problem is, Fred never *did* that.

ANDY (*cool, controlled, to* DEE). Hey. This is between me and Fred, okay? I'm here to see Fred.

DEE. So you can *punish* him some more.

ANDY (*cool, rationally*). He *deserves* to be punished.

DEE. He's *already* been punished.

ANDY. Really? Seems pretty comfortable to me. Sitting here, drinking his little – How is that *punishment*, huh? Who's the one whose life has been fucking destroyed? –   assumes "the one"

DEE *can't take it anymore. He busts up laughing.*

– Who's the one who's gotta go through the rest of their life in constant *fear* and *pain*?

DEE (*laughing*). Oh, you did *not*.

ANDY (*controlled*). Answer the question.

DEE (*to* FRED). Is that what he actually said?

ANDY. See? You can't answer.

DEE (*to* ANDY). Lemme understand this: So *your life was destroyed forever* cuzza something that happened on a piano bench when you was twelve years old?

ANDY (*controlled*). Fuck you.

DEE. That's why you come driving all this way? Taking a day off from your *bank* –

ANDY (*smug, calmly overlapping*). It's not a bank, okay? It's not a bank.

DEE (*continuous*). – c'mon honey, let's all take a trip downstate so I can tell some poor old white man sitting in a wheelchair living offa food stamps, tell him about all the *pain* I feel cuzza all the little *psychological problems* in my life? Honey, why'ntchoo shut up about your fuckin' problems? You don't know what a problem *is*. I could tell you tales of childhood would curl your toes, but I don't gotta be a little bitch about it, runnin' round resta my life cryin' to everybody about my tragic fuckin' childhood – baby, that's thirty *years ago*. Maybe it's 'bout fuckin' time you *moved on*.

ANDY *nods, controlled, jaw set.*

FRED (*carefully, looking at the contract*). Andy – It's true, I did do these first two things to you, but this third one is a thing I did to *Tommy* –

ANDY (*controlled*). And to me. You forced yourself on me.

FRED. – and I'll never forgive myself for that, and I admitted to it in court, so maybe you remembered hearing me say that and got a little mixed up on the details –

ANDY (*overlapping*). Nope. Nope. Nope.

FRED (*continuous*). – but this one thing is something I did to *Tommy*, and not to you. (*Beat.*) So I don't know why it is you want me to – ?

ANDY (*about to explode, but holding it in*). *Because it's true. Because. It's. Fucking* – I remember *every single detail* with absolute fucking clarity. And *you…* are not entitled to *question* that. victims can't be questioned

DEE (*casually*). Alright then. *I* got a question: Is Fred circumcised?

Pause. ANDY *stares.*

but who is are what process, here?

FRED (*sadly*). Ohhhh, don't.

DEE (*innocently*). I'm just sayin', if everything happened the way he says it did – (*To* ANDY.) then *I* would like to ask, does Fred – or does he not – have a *foreskin*?

FRED *sadly shakes his head.* ANDY *stares at* DEE, *furious, but unsure of the answer.*

Now of course, I happen to *know* the answer cuz I'm the one helping him in and outta the bathtub twice a week. Whereas you gotta retrieve it from your memory – which as you say, is *crystal*-clear –

FRED. This is wrong on so many levels.

DEE. – but see, that'd be a little detail I think I might be inclined to remember.

Pause. ANDY *shakes his head in barely suppressed rage. The door to* GIO's *room abruptly opens and* EFFIE *darts across the hall to the bathroom, closing the door behind her.* ANDY *very slowly folds his contract and returns it to the envelope.* FRED *reaches out to him sympathetically –*

ANDY (*pulling away, quietly controlled*). Don't ever touch me.

> ANDY *calmly stands, walks to the door, opens it quietly, exits, closing door behind him.* FRED *and* DEE *silently remain where they are.* FRED *sadly shakes his head.*

DEE (*quietly to* FRED). So was that a yes or a no?

> *Then* GIO *casually strolls out of his room, en route to kitchen.*

GIO (*as he passes through*). What happened to your friend, Fred?

> GIO *enters kitchen.* EFFIE *enters from bathroom, plops down at table.*

EFFIE. Omigod I had to pee so bad.

GIO. Felix still not back yet?

> *We hear a refrigerator open and close and* GIO *returns with an energy drink in a can. He surveys the room.* GIO *swigs from his can.*

Hey, Fred, how 'bout playin' some bridge? No good with two people but if we got three we could play cut-throat.

> EFFIE *takes a drag from a vape pen.* DEE *watches with alarm.* FRED *is lost in thought.*

Fred –

FRED (*very quietly*). No thank you.

EFFIE (*to* GIO). Can I have a Nutter Butter?

GIO. Ask Fred.

DEE (*to* EFFIE). Excuse me, please?

EFFIE (*to* FRED). Can I have a Nutter Butter?

DEE. Excuse me, young lady? May I ask what that is you're smoking?

EFFIE. Okay first of all it's not smoking it's juuling – ?

DEE (*to* GIO). Oh, you *cannot* be serious.

EFFIE. – and second of all?

DEE (*to* GIO). That better not be *weed oil* she's smoking in that little pipe. Is that what I'm smelling?

EFFIE. Okay, it's not smoking it's juuling – ?

DEE (*to* GIO). Are you and your little hoodrat friend actually *smoking weed* in this house – ?

GIO. I'm not smoking it.

DEE (*to* GIO). – are you outta your microscopic *mind*?

EFFIE. Can I explain something?

DEE (*to* EFFIE). Honey, I'm afraid we're gonna have to ask you to leave now –

EFFIE. But can I explain?

| DEE. – you don't need to explain, you just need to take that somewhere else. | EFFIE (*continuous*). Cuz I have a condition? It's called interstitial cystitis? |

EFFIE (*continuous*). – and CBD is the number-one recommended treatment pending approval from the FDA?

DEE (*re:* GIO). And let me explain something to *you*: (*Re:* GIO.) This young man is on the *sex offender registry*.

EFFIE. I know that.

GIO. She knows that.

DEE (*to* EFFIE). You know what that is?

EFFIE. So's my cousin Brianna.

DEE. Well, good for Brianna. But I don't think this is someone you wanna be on intimate terms with –

| GIO. Fuck you talking about *intimate terms* – ? | EFFIE (*re:* GIO). Ew. Gross. With *him*? |

GIO (*continuous*). – I ain't *fucking* this girl. Please. You think I can't do better'n that?

EFFIE (*to* GIO, *casually*). Fuck you.

DEE (*to* EFFIE). – and you can't be smoking that up in here, you understand me? Cuz you're about to get some folks ina whole lotta trouble –

GIO. No, the *trouble*, ya see, is *you* getting up in everybody *business*, and I believe I speak for the household when I say we are getting a little *tired* of your bullshit –

DEE. Young lady?

GIO (*to* EFFIE). – walkin' around here acting like his shit don't smell – I come off smellin' like *roses* next to the shit this motherfucker done.

DEE (*to* EFFIE). You take that outta here.

GIO (*to* EFFIE, *re:* DEE). Know what he did? This man right here?

EFFIE (*annoyed*). I don't *care*.

GIO. Google it. Google Desmond Malcolm Motley. Had homosexual relations with a adolescent teenage *boy* –

EFFIE (*defending* DEE). *So?*

GIO. – wanna know what happened to that boy?

FRED (*quietly*). Gio?

GIO. Know where that boy is today?

EFFIE (*to* GIO *re:* DEE). Leave him *alone*.

GIO. That boy contracted the HIV virus, *died of AIDS*.

EFFIE (*beat, hand to heart, sympathetic to* DEE). Omi*god*.

FRED. Gio?

GIO. Wound up *dead* at the age of twenty-three. Look it up.

EFFIE (*to* DEE, *sympathetically*). That's so sad.

FRED (*slowly*). Gio? Dee is HIV negative, and you know that as well as I do –

GIO. How do I know that?

FRED. – and you know he never hurt that boy –

FRED	GIO. Didn't *hurt*	EFFIE (*to* GIO).
(*continuous*). –	him? Boy's	Why are you
and you have no	*dead*, Fred.	being such an
right to say such	Seems hurt to	asshole? He
horrible things	me. I mean,	didn't do
and I'm getting	how much more	anything to you.
very tired of all	hurt you think	
of this	he's gonna get?	
meanness –		

FRED (*continuous, exploding*). *– and I want it to stop right now!!*

EFFIE (*quietly*). God.

All stop and turn. FRED *never loses his temper.*

FRED. *You have no idea what Dee has been through, and you're just making up lies to hurt his feelings, as if life isn't hard enough without us being deliberately hurtful and cruel to each other.* (*Quieter.*) And I'm sorry to raise my voice, but I think maybe you owe Dee an apology.

Front door opens. All turn. ANDY *is back.*

ANDY. Can somebody move that car please?

All are taken aback by the non-sequitur.

GIO (*quietly to* FRED *and* DEE). Whatzy talking about?

ANDY. Whose car is that?

FRED (*confused*). *What's* the matter?

ANDY. Chevy Cavalier?

EFFIE. What about it?

ANDY. Is that yours?

EFFIE. Yeah?

ANDY. Can you move it, please?

EFFIE. Am I blocking you?

ANDY. Yes you are.

EFFIE. Sorry.

ANDY. Thank you.

> EFFIE *jumps up, exits out front door.* GIO *intercepts* ANDY *before he can follow, pulling out wallet and business card.*

GIO (*privately*). 'Scuse me, sir? Sir? Sir?

ANDY. Yeah?

GIO (*privately sycophantic*). If I could take two seconds of your time?

ANDY. Yeah?

GIO. Don't mean to waylay ya – just wanted to give ya this real quick and maybe next time you're in the area I could buy ya a cup of coffee, maybe pick yer brain about small-business startups in the Chicago area, that sorta thing? (*Re: card.*) And that's me – Giovanni Joseph – and that's the office number and a home phone for evening hours – I don't have a smartphone at present but I do get voicemail so if you just hang onto that and you can gimme one of yours, if you gotta card on you – ?

ANDY. No.

GIO. – or email it. And that's the email for the Staples – so if ya put my name in the subject line I'll get the message one way or another – (*Offering hand.*) and I want to say it's been a pleasure talking to ya –

ANDY (*vaguely accepting*). Uh-huh.

GIO. – cuz I don't often get the opportunity to make acquaintances of a professional nature, especially in a town this size –

ANDY (*with calm finality*). Excuse me – Sorry – Um. I don't have any idea who you are, okay? –

GIO. Well, that's what I'm –

ANDY (*continuous*). – and I have no interest in whatever it is you're talking about – but I do want to say one thing – (*To* FRED *and* DEE, *trying to be rational.*) Because people like you, okay? With your, I dunno, your orientation, or or or predilection, or whatever – it's a *sickness*, okay? And I understand that, and I even have some sympathy for it, believe it or not, but I honestly can't even begin to comprehend how any person – how any human being could ever look at a *defenseless* – *Ever* – (*Re:* DEE.) I mean, this person's *not even ashamed of what he did.* (*Beat.*) And I don't understand how that's possible. I really don't. Cuz if you don't feel *shame*, see – If a person doesn't feel *shame*? – *mersault*

FRED (*overlapping*). I'm *very* ashamed, Andy.

ANDY (*continuous*). – or maybe you lack the basic human capacity for compassion or or or or empathy – Cuz otherwise you wouldn't be *questioning* a victim's – Cuz *victims don't lie*, okay? Victims tell the truth. And if you don't have *empathy* for that? Then I'm not sure you're entitled to call yourself – cuz when an *animal* harms a human, ya know, that animal is put down. And I'm not saying that, but there happens to be a majority of people out there who believe that, yeah, people like you should probably – at very least? Be made to experience some small fraction of – and I don't believe in torture? But rape is a form of torture, *too*, okay? And if tomorrow the laws were changed, and that was the result? If you were forced to undergo even *two seconds* of what we went through…? (*Beat.*) I wouldn't have a problem with that. I really wouldn't. So.

(Handwritten margin notes: "← see scotts boys", "blatant dehumanization")

EFFIE *has quietly returned to the front door.*

EFFIE. Does anybody have any jumper cables?

  ANDY *exhales, shakes his head.*

GIO *(quietly)*. Whatzit, the battery?

EFFIE. Maybe?

GIO. You try the ignition?

EFFIE. Yeah.

GIO. What's it doin'?

EFFIE. It's like click click click.

GIO. Maybe the alternator.

EFFIE *(to* ANDY*)*. Do *you* have jumper cables?

ANDY *(calmly)*. I do not have jumper cables.

GIO *(to* EFFIE*)*. *You* don't got jumper cables?

EFFIE. Why would I have jumper cables?

GIO. Everybody's got jumper cables.

EFFIE. Well I don't have jumper cables.

GIO. Ya check your trunk?

EFFIE. It's a hatchback.

GIO. Ya check your hatchback?

EFFIE. I *don't. Have. Jumper cables.*

GIO. How can a person not have jumper cables?

EFFIE *(defending herself)*. *You* don't have jumper cables.

GIO. Cuz I don't got a *car*.

ANDY. Okay. I don't give a shit. Just put the car in neutral and roll it into the fuckin' street, alright? I just want it out of the way.

GIO. Whoa.

EFFIE *(taken aback, hurt)*. *Sorry.*

GIO (*awkward beat, then*). Sir, I am truly sorry for –

ANDY. No no no no no. I don't want your apology. I just want
it solved.

Pause.

GIO. Huh. Ummm. Ya know what – we got another resident,
he's in the automotive field, he's gotta have some jumper
cables, if ya want me to – ?

ANDY. Fine.

ANDY *turns to exit. Before he can leave:*

FRED. Andy?

ANDY. What?

FRED. Your phone?

DEE *snorts.* ANDY*'s phone is still plugged into the outlet.
He crosses to retrieve it:*

DEE (*quietly*). Yeah, that's right. Don't wanna 'forget' that a
second time.

FRED. Sh sh sh –   On forgetfulness

ANDY *stops, glares at* DEE.

ANDY. What the fuck's that supposed to – ?

FRED. Nothing.

DEE (*to* FRED). He didn't 'forget' that *phone*. He just wanted
to come back and see ya without his wife tagging along.

ANDY (*calmly macho threat*). Uh-huh. Uh-huh. You know, one
of the first things you learn in our group is how not to
respond to that kind of bullshit.

DEE. Tell ya what, Fred. You must give one helluva blowjob.
He keeps coming back for more.

ANDY *grabs the baseball bat next to the front door and
swings at a table lamp, breaking it, then advances on* DEE,
who remains defiantly calm. EFFIE *turns on the camera of
her phone and begins recording.*

ANDY	FRED. No	DEE	GIO. Whoa	EFFIE
(advancing on DEE). What'd I say to you, dude, huh? Don't fuck with me, okay? Cuz I will fucking take you down.	no no no – Andy? Andy? He didn't mean anything. That's just the way he jokes sometimes – Andy? Andy?	*(amused, non-confrontational).* Well, wasn't *that* a dramatic gesture. Now we're getting closer to the bone of contention.	whoa whoa. Sir. Sir. Sir. Let's not resort to violence. That's never gonna solve the problem.	*(narrating video).* Omigod. *Oh. My. God.* That man just smashed this lamp and now – *OMIGOD* – he's threatening this *other* man – ?

FRED *reaches out, touches* ANDY.

FRED (*calmly*). – please just don't hurt anybody.

★ ANDY. *DON'T YOU FUCKING TOUCH ME –*

ANDY *moves to strike* FRED, *then grabs him roughly, pulls him out of his wheelchair and onto the floor.* EFFIE *screams.* GIO *tries to restrain* ANDY *from behind as* DEE *grabs a dumbbell and brandishes it at* ANDY, *defending* FRED.

ANDY	FRED.	DEE. Get	GIO. No no	EFFIE.
(out of control). I NEVER HURT ANYONE IN MY FUCK- ING LIFE!	Okay. Okay. I'm okay. It's okay, Andy. No one's going to hurt you.	your fuckin' ass outta this house, mother- fucker. Get the fuck	no no no. Whoa whoa don't do that. Can't do that. Can't start	OMI- GOD!! He attacked the old man!!! *(To* ANDY.) *This is*

YOU	Every-	outta	hurting	*a safe*
ARE	body's	here	people.	*space!*
THE	okay.	before	Whoa	*This is*
ONE		I crack	whoa	*a safe*
THAT		your	whoa.	*space!!*
HURT		skull		
PEOPLE		wide		
YOU		open and		
MOTH-		I will do		
ER-FUC		it, too.		
-KING				
SONOFA				
BITCH –				

"the victim"
(one)

ANDY (*out of control*). *YOU ARE NOT THE VICTIM!!! I AM THE VICTIM! I AM THE VICTIM! I AM THE VIC–* (*To* GIO.) *get your fucking hands off of me.*

ANDY *disentangles himself from* GIO, *flings bat aside, tries to calm himself.*

GIO (*releasing* ANDY). – alright alright that's cool – you're the victim, bruh. You're the victim. Whatever you say.

Long pause. Everybody on high alert.

EFFIE (*almost inaudibly, still recording*). Omigod I just got that on video.

ANDY (*subdued, out of breath*)....now, will somebody get the fuckin' jumper cables please?

DEE. Fuck your jumper cables.

GIO. No no no no no I'm getting the jumper cables. And we're all gonna stay calm and stay cool and focused and everybody's gonna stay right where they are, and we're gonna get the jumper cables and you'll be on your way, alright? –

GIO *opens* FELIX*'s door as he talks, keeping his eyes on the room, in case violence erupts again:*

– cuz violence is never the answer. Psalms Eleven-Five: The Lord is on His heavenly throne, and He loves the righteous, but the lover of violence is wicked unto His sight –

The door is open – The others stand frozen, staring. EFFIE *puts her hand over her mouth and silently runs out the front door:*

What?

GIO *turns –* FELIX *has hanged himself from a light fixture in his room, a belt around his neck, a plastic bag over his head, dressed only in boxer shorts and a T-shirt. He has shit himself and his skin is gray. An overturned chair at his feet.*

FRED. Ohhhhhh Felix.

Everybody stands in silence for a moment or two, then DEE *crosses and slowly pulls the accordion door closed. From outside, the flashing lights of a police car. A police radio crackles. Lights slowly transition to dawn.* ANDY *exits.* DEE *returns* FRED *to his chair. When the transition is complete,* DEE *and* FRED *are seated quietly at the table, eyes downcast.* FRED *holds a damp cloth to his cheek.* GIO *sits in a corner by the door, wrists cuffed behind his back.*

IVY *enters talking on a cellphone.*

IVY (*into phone*). Forty-three eighty-six copy that just givin' you a heads-up I gotta impounded vehicle comin' your way – that's right, yes ma'am, so I needa make sure we gotta receiving officer on duty? Thank you, ma'am. And we're gonna need protective service on call cuz I gotta potential ten-fifty with a juvenile –

EFFIE *stands at the front door, wildly distraught, tearful, mascara smudging her cheeks.*

EFFIE. *Can I at least have my phone back please???*

IVY. No, ma'am, you may not.

EFFIE. Omigod will you not even let me *explain*?

IVY. Young lady?

EFFIE. You won't even *listen*?

IVY. Wait in the car, please?

EFFIE (*holding up a card*). This is my registry card and my doctor's license, and her name is Doctor Jeanine Epperson, and I have interstitial cystitis, which is a recognized treatable condition under Illinois statute HB1 –

IVY (*to phone*). Gimme a second.

EFFIE (*continuous*). – and I am legally entitled to possess two-point-seven-five liquid ounces for my own personal use, and I am a free inhabitant of this territory –

A uniformed FEMALE COP *approaches* EFFIE *at the door.* IVY *gestures for her to take* EFFIE *away.*

(*As she is led out.*) – and you cannot abridge my rights under the Fourth Amendment and you need to learn how to do your fucking job – (*From off, losing her shit at the* FEMALE COP.) *cuz I do not consent to this detention!! I do not consent!! I do not consent!!!!! Help me!!! I do not consent!* (*Etc.*)

After a car-door slam, silence. GIO *speaks to himself, no one listening, as* EM *appears at front door, speaking to* IVY.

GIO (*philosophically*). Well well well.

EM (*frustrated, from door*). Excuse me?

GIO. Let's all have a good long look at this scenario, shall we?

EM. Hello?

GIO. If this don't more or less epitomize the dysfunctional state of what passes for justice in this pitiful excuse for a country.

The sliding door opens – FELIX *is gone and the mattress has been stripped of its linens. A* MALE COP *hauls out two large garbage bags, leaving the door open behind him, and exiting out the front door.*

✣ EM (*to* IVY). Can anybody give me an answer, please?

IVY. What's the question?

EM (*entering*). The question is how much longer we're
expected to sit out there.

IVY. Almost done.

EM. Okay so what does that mean? Does that mean five
minutes? Does it mean half an hour?

As EM *talks, another* MALE COP *leads a drug-detection
dog on a leash into the main room, sniffing at the walls and
furniture. The* COP *hands off a Ziploc evidence bag to* IVY,
continuing out the front door with the dog.

Because I'm sorry, but I have a child who is in *alone* in a
hotel room right now, with no one but a *babysitter* – ?

IVY. I understand that.

EM (*continuous*). – and if this continues much *longer*? I'm
going to take down your name and badge number –

IVY (*into phone*). Call you right back.

EM. – because you cannot detain someone without warrant for
defending himself against a convicted predator.

IVY. Ma'am? Your husband came here of his own free will –

IVY. – which neither of y'all   EM. *My husband did nothing*
had any call to be doing in   *wrong.*
the first place –
      new character of Andy would insist he's
      of Andy   *due this...*
      sympathetic

IVY. – and ya can't go striking elderly individuals in the face,
or threaten 'em with a baseball bat –

EM (*calmly*). So this is harassment.   *invocation of legal terminology*

IVY (*continuous*). – cuz that's called aggravated assault, alright?

EM. *My husband is innocent.*

IVY. If you'll wait outside, please?

EM (*turns, walks away*). This is shameful.

EM *exits out the front door.* GIO *talks to himself, no one
listening.*

GIO. Who's the man once said the arc of the moral universe is long but it bends toward justice?

The first MALE COP *arrives at the door, talks to* IVY.

Problem with that, see, if ya remember your high-school geometry, an arc's just one part of a larger circle, so sooner or later ya wind up right the fuck back where ya started from.

IVY *gestures for the* COP *to take* GIO *away.*

GIO *stands to exit, talking to the room – or possibly to us – as he exits.*

But I'm not bitter. Ephesians Four Thirty-one: Let bitterness and wrath be put away from ye; and be ye kind to one another, and tenderhearted and forgiving, even as He in Christ's name has forgiven you. And y'all can quote me on that. Amen and goodnight.

GIO *and the* COP *are gone.*

IVY. Everybody alright?

FRED. We're fine.

EM *briskly returns, pocketbook in hand. She enters the room, placing money on the table before* FRED *and* DEE.

EM (*to* FRED *and* DEE). Okay, and this is a hundred dollars? Which I think should more than cover the cost of your lamp? And I'm sorry for what your friend did to himself? But I do have to say? Because I am not a vengeful or spiteful person? So I'm sorry if it comes out sounding that way, but I do have to say I think possibly he made the right decision –
incredibly cruel
FRED *and* DEE *do not respond in any way.*

– because there is a *change* taking place, okay? And it's long overdue, and people have been silent for too long, and I don't claim to have all the answers, and I've certainly never believed in, like, an afterlife or anything? But now I'm actually kind of hoping there *is* one, because I don't think we have the right kind of punishment for people who've done things like you've done, in this life, and maybe in the next
conflation of speaking/ being heard/ saying one's peace + wanting (or believing one's entitled to) see the other person suffer

one some kind of higher power will be able to figure that out. And I'm sorry if that sounds harsh? But that's the way I feel.

EM *shoulders her purse and exits.* FRED *and* DEE *remain behind,* IVY *at the door.*

IVY (*carefully*). So... I'll be back later on, get a statement from both of ya but if y'all could do me a favor and help start clearing out these rooms? I can get a decon team in on Wednesday but if y'all'd maybe get a headstart boxin' up some of this stuff – ?

FRED. Okay.

IVY. – appreciate it. And maybe we'll see about getting a coupla new residents in here, maybe end of next week.

FRED. Okay.

IVY. Alright. So maybe two-thirty, three o'clock. If y'all get those boxes together in the meantime.

FRED. We can do that.

IVY (*beat*). Real sorry about Felix.

Long pause. FRED *and* DEE *don't respond.*

Anyway.

IVY *exits, closing the door behind her.* FRED *and* DEE *remain at the table. Long silence.*

FRED. I don't think we *have* any boxes, do we?

DEE. I'll get some at the IGA.

FRED. Not the IGA.

DEE (*remembering*). Not the IGA.

FRED. Maybe Big Lots.

DEE (*beat, re:* FRED*'s cheek*). Still bleeding?

FRED (*shakes his head*). I think he musta caught me with his wedding ring.

DEE. Oughta put some Neosporin on that.

FRED. Probably a good idea.

Pause. FRED *looks at* DEE*'s poster, still leaning against the wall*.

Shame about that poster.

DEE. Thank you, Fred.

FRED. Can you replace it?

DEE (*shakes his head*). Collector's item.

FRED. Maybe a little Scotch tape?

DEE. We could try.

Pause. FRED *looks at poster*.

FRED. I don't think I ever saw that movie.

DEE. Got it on Blu-ray.

FRED. I should watch that one of these days.

DEE (*beat*). Miss Ross got nominated Best Actress.

FRED. Is that right?

DEE (*affirmative*). Mm-hmm.

FRED. Did she win?

DEE (*negative*). Hm-mm.

FRED. Aww.

DEE. Liza Minnelli for *Cabaret*.

FRED (*beat*). Well, she was good, too.

DEE. Very good.

FRED. It's a musical isn't it? Musical comedy?

DEE. More of a tragicomedy.

[handwritten: first conversation in the play about second repair]

[handwritten: metatheatrical device – debating about this play.]

FRED. What year was that?

DEE. 1972.

FRED. 1972. (*Beat, factually.*) I was in the navy.

DEE. It was at the Embassy Theatre in downtown Fort Wayne and my cousin Rhonda snuck me in through the back door because the tickets were two dollars and fifty cents and we only had four dollars and a Kit Kat bar. And we sat there in the dark, and when they got to the scene where Billie's a junkie and they take her to jail and throw her in that padded cell and she's lying there all alone…

DEE *nearly cries, covers his face.* FRED *reaches out, touches him.*

FRED. Ohhh, now. It's okay. Shhhhh.

DEE (*ashamed*). I don't think I'm a very good person, Fred.

FRED. Ohhh, stop. Why would you say something like that…?

DEE. I'm filled with so much anger and hatred and it gets the better of me sometimes and I say things I shouldn't say so I'm sorry if I did.

FRED. Well. I think you can be forgiven for that.

Pause. DEE *recovers as best he can.*

DEE. I can make coffee if you want.

FRED. Probably oughta get some sleep.

DEE. I don't think I can sleep.

FRED. Well. Maybe we'll just sit here for a little bit, then.

DEE. I'm gonna have one of your Nutter Butters.

FRED. Have as many as you want.

DEE *eats a cookie. Silence.*

(*Beat.*) Would it be alright with you if I played some music?

DEE. I wouldn't mind that.

FRED. Are you sure?

DEE. That'd be nice.

FRED. Alright then.

> FRED *wheels himself over to the CD player and his little keyboard.*

Anything special you'd like me to play?

DEE. Whatever you feel like.

> FRED *selects a CD, inserts it.*

FRED. And after this, maybe we'll sleep.

DEE. That sounds like a plan.

> FRED *presses play –* Chopin*'s 'Prelude Op. 28, No. 7' begins, and* FRED *silently plays along as* DEE *eats his cookie. Lights slowly fade as music concludes.*

> *End of play.*

www.nickhernbooks.co.uk

facebook.com/nickhernbooks

twitter.com/nickhernbooks